O9-CFT-639

*Twayne's United States Authors Series*

Sylvia E. Bowman, *Editor*

INDIANA UNIVERSITY

*Edward Dahlberg*

# EDWARD DAHLBERG

By FRED MORAMARCO
*San Diego State College*

 206

Twayne Publishers, Inc. :: New York

Library of Congress Catalog Card Number: 75-187606

MANUFACTURED IN THE UNITED STATES OF AMERICA

Dedicated to the memory
of my mother,
Nina Moramarco,
and to
Sheila, Stephen and Nicholas

# Preface

Writing a book about a living author is always a hazardous venture. When that author's name is Edward Dahlberg, the hazards are considerably multiplied. Those who know his work well do not question Dahlberg's considerable accomplishment as a man of letters. As the author of two acknowledged masterpieces (*Can These Bones Live* and *Because I Was Flesh*) and of many other works which bear the mark of a distinctly individual prose stylist, it would seem easy to justify a full-length study of his work. The fact that this book is the first lengthy survey of the Dahlberg canon to appear in print is indicative of the caution with which critics have approached the man; for Dahlberg has been unusually severe on those commentators who have written about his work with anything less than almost total adulation. A master of invective, he has condemned the writers of these critiques, challenged their morality, and cast aspersions on their motives. The result of this attitude has been a polarization on the part of critics who write about Dahlberg. He is seen either as the most neglected genius of our time or as an arrogant pedant. Neither approach, it seems to me, casts very much light on Dahlberg's substantial literary achievement.

My intention in this book is to take something of a middle way between these two extremes. My admiration for Dahlberg's writing will, I am sure, be evident. However, this admiration stops short of the assumption that Dahlberg can do no wrong. It seems apparent to me that some of Dahlberg's fourteen books are more effective than others: some will survive our own time, and others will not. Thus, the question that is implicit throughout this investigation is "What are those qualities of Dahlberg's writing which separate his best work from his minor efforts?" Or, to put it more specifically, "Why is *Because I Was Flesh* a more effective and affecting book than either *Those Who Perish* or *The Flea of Sodom*?"

The answers to these questions are not easy, but I think they will emerge from a careful reading of Dahlberg's work in its entirety, from his early "proletarian" novels through his later excursions into mythology and autobiography. The phrase "careful reading" captures exactly my intention throughout, for it is my belief that this is the foundation of all worthwhile criticism. I approach Dahlberg's work neither as a psychological, mythological, historical, biographical, nor as moralistic critic but as a "careful reader" who, ideally, draws from all of these traditions.

My debt to Harold Billings is very great, as it must be for anyone who writes about Edward Dahlberg. Mr. Billings knows more about Dahlberg's life and work than anyone else I know, and he has been exceedingly generous in all my correspondence with him. Let me thank him here particularly for supplying the details of the Chronology which precedes the text, and for his many helpful suggestions regarding the manuscript. I am also indebted to Ken Eble and Ed Lueders for their careful reading of the manuscript and for their very valuable suggestions. To Steve Baar, Stan Cook, and Bill Sullivan, my colleagues, I am thankful for the considerable encouragement they provided me from the inception of this work to its completion.

Edward Dahlberg himself, it is impossible to sufficiently acknowledge, except to say that this entire book is an acknowledgment of his work. The experience of meeting with him and corresponding with him has made my task considerably more rewarding.

Finally, my thanks as always to my wife Sheila, who makes everything possible.

# Acknowledgments

For permission to quote from Edward Dahlberg's published works, I am grateful to:

City Lights Books, for *Bottom Dogs* (Copyright © 1930, 1961 by Edward Dahlberg).

New Directions Publishing Corporation, for *Can These Bones Live* (Copyright © 1941 by New Directions. Copyright © 1960 by Edward Dahlberg); *Because I Was Flesh* (Copyright © 1963 by Edward Dahlberg); *The Edward Dahlberg Reader* (Introduction by Paul Carroll, Copyright © 1967 by New Directions).

Horizon Press, for *Truth Is More Sacred* (Copyright © 1961 by Sir Herbert Read and Edward Dahlberg); *Reasons of the Heart* (Copyright © 1965 by Edward Dahlberg).

University of Minnesota Press, for *Alms for Oblivion* (Copyright © 1964 by the University of Minnesota Press).

George Braziller, Inc., for *Epitaphs of Our Time* (Copyright © 1967 by Edward Dahlberg); *The Confessions of Edward Dahlberg* (Copyright © 1971 by Edward Dahlberg).

Weybright and Talley, Inc., for *The Carnal Myth* (Copyright © 1968 by Edward Dahlberg).

Roger Beacham, for *The Leafless American* (Copyright © 1967 by Edward Dahlberg); *Edward Dahlberg, American Ishmael of Letters* (Copyright © 1968 by Harold Billings).

In addition, I am of course thankful to Edward Dahlberg himself for permission to use material he sent to me in letters, and to quote from *Those Who Perish, From Flushing to Calvary, The Flea of Sodom, The Sorrows of Priapus,* and *Cinpango's Hinder Door.*

# Contents

# Chronology

1900 Edward Dalberg (spelling later changed) born July 22,
1900, in a charity hospital in Boston, the son of Elizabeth
Dalberg and Saul Gottdank.

1901– Travels with his mother to London, Dallas, Memphis, New
1905 Orleans, Louisville, and Denver.

1905– Lizzie settles with her son in Kansas City where she oper-
1906 ates the Star Lady Barbershop at Sixteen East Eighth
Street.

1907– Edward in Catholic orphanage in Kansas City.
1908

1912– Edward an inmate of the Jewish Orphan Asylum in Cleve-
1917 land.

1917– Works as messenger boy for Western Union in Cleveland
1921 and in Kansas City stockyards; a hobo in the West; a pri-
vate in the United States Army; lives in Los Angeles.

1922– Attends University of California, Berkeley.
1923

1924– Attends Columbia University; takes bachelor of science
1925 degree in philosophy.

1926 Teaches at James Madison High School, New York.

1926– Lives in Paris, Monte Carlo, Brussels. Writes *Bottom Dogs*
1928 after several novels are discarded. Changes spelling of
name.

1929 First part of *Bottom Dogs* published as "Beginnings and
Continuations of Lorry Gilchrist" in *This Quarter* No. 4.
(Issue also includes two poems, a short story, and an
essay.) *Bottom Dogs* published in London.

1930 *Bottom Dogs* published in New York.

1931 Contributes to *Poetry* and *Pagany*.

1932 *From Flushing to Calvary*. *Kentucky Blue Grass Henry
Smith* (Part 6 of preceding title) published in an edition

of ninety-five copies. Contributes to *The Nation* and *The New Republic.*

1933 *From Flushing to Calvary* published in London. Visits Berlin at time of Reichstag fire.

1934 Anti-Nazi novel *Those Who Perish.*

1935 Helps organize the first American Writers' Congress; presents paper, "Fascism and Writers."

1936 Portion of uncompleted novel, "Bitch Goddess," published in *Signature* magazine.

1937–1940 Dahlberg variously in New York, Mexico City, San Antonio, Kansas City, Chicago, Boston, Washington, New Orleans, Los Angeles. Works on *Do These Bones Live.*

1941 *Do These Bones Live.*

1942 Marries Winifred Sheehan Moore, mother of his sons Geoffrey and Joel.

1947 *Sing O Barren* (a revision of *Do These Bones Live*) published in London.

1950 *The Flea of Sodom* published in London; sheets imported by New Directions for American edition. Marries R'Lene LaFleur Howell.

1950–1953 Lives in New York, Berkeley, Topanga, California, Santa Monica. Contributes regularly to *Tomorrow* and *The Freeman.*

1953–1956 Lives in Santa Monica and Berkeley.

1956–1957 Travels to Bornholm, Malaga, Ascona, Paris, Mallorca.

1957 *The Sorrows of Priapus* published by New Directions.

1958–1964 Lives in Mallorca, New York, Dublin.

1960 *Can These Bones Live* revised, reissued. Dahlberg receives award from Longview Foundation for a section of *Because I Was Flesh* published in *Big Table.*

1961 *Truth Is More Sacred* (with Sir Herbert Read) published by Routledge & Paul, London, and Horizon Press. Dahlberg receives grant from National Institute of Arts and Letters.

1964 *Because I Was Flesh* published by New Directions. *Alms for Oblivion* published by University of Minnesota Press.

1965 Dahlberg returns to Kansas City from Mallorca as Professor of English Literature at University of Missouri; *Reasons of the Heart* published by Horizon Press; receives grant from Rockefeller Foundation.

1966 *Cinpango's Hinder Door.*

1967 *Epitaphs of Our Times; The Edward Dahlberg Reader;* and *The Leafless American.* Marries Julia Lawlor.

1968 *The Carnal Myth.* Elected to National Institute of Arts and Letters. Sails for Dublin. Returns to New York to begin work on *The Confessions,* a sequel to *Because I Was Flesh.*

1970 A *Festschrift* for Edward Dahlberg published in *TriQuarterly.*

1971 *The Confessions of Edward Dahlberg* published by Braziller. Moves to Sarasota, Florida.

## CHAPTER *1*

# The Transformation of a Man

UNTIL the mid 1960's, the few readers who knew the name Edward Dahlberg generally associated it with the proletarian literature of the 1930's. Dahlberg was the writer who gave the name to the "bottom dog" literature of the depression years; and, along with his Marxist-oriented peers, he aimed to place literature in the service of the proletariat. This view even then was misleading, for to call Dahlberg a proletarian novelist on the basis of his first two novels is stretching the definition of the term. In the 1970's, however, the view is not only misleading but very far from being a description of Dahlberg's literary orientation. Consequently, when the name Dahlberg is brought up today, few mention his "proletarian" works; instead, he is considered a stormy iconoclast, a stylistic genius, or an eccentric literary anachronism, depending upon the speaker's, or the writer's, opinion of his work.

Thus, when we discuss Edward Dahlberg the writer, it is important to know *which* Edward Dahlberg we are talking about, for his literary development covers a period of over forty years from the publication of *Bottom Dogs* in 1929 to that of the second part of his memories *The Confessions of Edward Dahlberg,* published in 1971. One of those writers whose creative powers seem to continually grow, he provides in each of his books additional evidence of a truly original, eloquent literary talent. Today, Dahlberg is something of a cult writer; and, though the cult is widening each year, he still writes for the "fit audience though few" that Milton sought.

There can be no question that the 1960's saw a remarkable enhancement of Dahlberg's literary reputation. His autobiography *Because I Was Flesh* was nominated for the National Book Award in 1964; he has been the recipient of Rockefeller and Longview Grants; and he received in 1967 the accolade of an *Edward Dahl-*

*berg Reader* published by New Directions. The following year saw the publications of *Edward Dahlberg: American Ishmael of Letters,* a book of essays devoted to his work; and in the same year he was elected to membership in the National Institute of Arts and Letters. In 1970, a long-awaited *Festschrift* for Edward Dahlberg was edited by Jonathan Williams for the prestigious literary review, *TriQuarterly;* and, though it is too early to tell, the publication of Dahlberg's *Confessions* seems certain to enhance his stature as one of our few literary originals.

Though Dahlberg has disparaged "originality" throughout most of his life and has particularly attacked the modernistic fetish to "make it new" that has characterized much of the literature of this century, it seems to me that much of his achievement falls squarely within the confines of the "modernist" temper. Like the writers he so thoroughly despises—Ezra Pound and T. S. Eliot, for example—he is driven by the need to relate his work to an historical tradition. Again and again we are reminded in Dahlberg's work of the familiar exhortation of T. S. Eliot: "the historical sense compels a man to write not merely with his own generation in his bones, but with a feeling that the whole of the literature of Europe from Homer and within it the whole of the literature of his own country has a simultaneous existence and composes a simultaneous order." [1]

Dahlberg's incredible assimilation of the literary traditions of the past has led him to what is perhaps his most important accomplishment: the creation of new generic forms which, as Ihab Hassan notes, exist "in that unchartered region between the novel, the essay, and the fable." [2] *The Flea of Sodom, The Sorrows of Priapus,* and *The Carnal Myth* are books which defy traditional classification, but they are major contributions to the history and development of literary types in the twentieth century. They emphasize the universality and permanence of myth, and they make available to us a vast body of native American rituals and legends which existed in our Pre-Columbian period. The repository of native lore in these works makes us aware "that the woes and the myths of a Chipewayan Indian are as extraordinary as the tragedy of Ceres." [3]

Dahlberg's interest in and study of mythology shaped his writing after 1940. His literary criticism, for example, moves away from the narrow confines of an academic approach, infused as it is with a broad spectrum of reading in ancient literatures. *Can These Bones Live* is a remarkable example of criticism that is as creative as D. H. Lawrence's *Studies in Classic American Literature,* or as William Carlos Williams' *In the American Grain.* Like its generic predecessors, Dahlberg's book reveals the author's heart and temperament as much as it illuminates the literature it analyzes. Mythological influences are also responsible for the reshaping of the material in *Bottom Dogs* and in *From Flushing to Calvary* in a nonfictional mode. *Because I Was Flesh* is a reexamination of the drab world presented in the earlier novels; but this time it is presented with a rich and allusive prose style—one which reflects Dahlberg's continuing attempt to make the writing of prose the art it was in the age of Elizabeth I. A few sentences from the opening pages of that work should suggest the impact of the study of myth on the later work and the degree to which it shapes the style: "Kansas City was my Tarsus; the Kaw and the Missouri Rivers were the washpots of joyous Dianas from St. Joseph and Joplin. It was a young, seminal town and the seed of its men were strong. Homer sang of many sacred towns in Hellas which were no better than Kansas City, as hilly as Eteonus and as stony as Aulis."[4] It is indeed superfluous to note that this is not proletarian, Naturalistic writing; it is that of a Classicist steeped in the cultural heritage of the Western world.

## I *The Life*

When Edward Dahlberg was born in a Boston charity hospital on July 22, 1900, he was given the surname of his mother Lizzie, as she was deserted by his father, Saul Gottdank, a vagabond barber, shortly before his birth. Lizzie took the infant Edward to England where she worked in London as a domestic servant. She had hoped to inherit money from a relative who had recently died there, but she was disappointed to discover that he had left most of his money to a Protestant church. Lizzie saved enough working as a scrubwoman and as a parlormaid to return with the child to the United States. Shortly thereafter, she became reunited with the boy's father (they had never been married—as Dahlberg describes it in his autobiography he was "as illegitimate as the pismire . . ."[5])—and together they opened a barber shop in Dallas,

Texas. Lizzie learned the barber's trade from Saul; and, as he gradually withdrew from the joint enterprise, he left her with most of the responsibility.

After several arguments about Saul's drawing money from the business to spend it on various women, Lizzie took the boy with her to Memphis. She worked as a door-to-door saleswoman for a brief period until Saul arrived in town and convinced her to join him in New Orleans and open a new barber shop. This second collaboration was even less successful than the first, and after Saul's third desertion, Lizzie traveled to Louisville and Denver with the boy, finally settling in Kansas City, where she went to work as a lady-barber.

Not discouraged by the failure of her previous business enterprises, Lizzie obtained a loan to open The Star Lady Barbershop on East Eighth Street in Kansas City. Within two years, Saul once again arrived in town, this time to claim his "half-share" of their original business venture in Dallas. Saul claimed that the partnership had never been dissolved, and Lizzie agreed to pay his claim in order to be finally rid of him.

This same year (1907) she underwent a serious operation and was forced to send Edward to a Catholic orphanage while she recuperated. Within a year she was once again able to take care of the young Edward and to remove him from the orphanage. The next few years of their life together were plagued by ill health and by increasing financial problems. Lizzie, determined to find a husband to help ease her burden, doggedly sought the comfort of marriage in her middle age. At the suggestion of one of her suitors, a Missouri River boat captain, she sent the boy away to the Jewish Orphan Asylum in Cleveland where he spent his adolescent years.

Dahlberg's life in the orphanage had an immeasurable impact upon his later years. The almost inhuman discipline of existence there is vividly described, novelistically in *Bottom Dogs* and *From Flushing to Calvary,* and autobiographically in *Because I Was Flesh.* In a letter to Robert M. Hutchins, Dahlberg writes, "I have always been loyal to my beginnings, by which I mean I have always been an orphan." [6] Perhaps this experience accounts for the intense bitterness of much of his writings as well as for his continual insistence that the separation of human beings from one another is the source of all our woe. These years have been memorialized in his work, and perhaps that is some consolation; but the traumatic effect they must have had on an impressionable young man of artistic inclination is impossible to determine.

From this point on, the details of Dahlberg's life are less easily accessible. Information about the early years can be garnered from his autobiography; and, though that work does take us through February, 1946 (the death of Lizzie Dahlberg), the latter chapters deal almost exclusively with his mother and tell us little about his literary development. Lacking a full-length biography, the best we can do is piece together bits and pieces about the later life from Dahlberg's letters and from the autobiographical essays in *Alms for Oblivion* and elsewhere. Of course, constructing a biographical sketch of a writer who is still living is always a delicate matter; therefore, we have to proceed cautiously.

Perhaps inheriting his wanderlust from both his parents, Dahlberg "hoboed" around the country after his dismissal from the orphanage at the age of seventeen. After a stint in the United States Army (an experience which Dahlberg never refers to in his writing), he attended the University of California at Berkeley ("when goats browsed near the campus"),[7] transferred to Columbia, and received a bachelor of science degree in philosophy there, specializing in the Pre-Socratic philosophers. Shortly after graduation, he taught high school for a year at James Madison High in New York.

In 1926, Dahlberg began his self-imposed exile in Europe and traveled widely on the Continent. A member of a literary clique in Paris, he associated primarily with Robert McAlmon, John Hermann, Richard Aldington, Hart Crane, and Ethel Moorehead. The latter, who was then editor of *This Quarter,* an expatriate literary magazine, was impressed enough by a short story Dahlberg submitted to the periodical to suggest that he try to write a novel. Taking Ethel Moorehead's suggestion, Dahlberg began work on *Bottom Dogs,* the first part of which was published in the Spring 1929 *This Quarter* as "The Beginnings and Continuations of Lorry Gilchrist."

Shortly after beginning *Bottom Dogs,* Dahlberg married for the first time. His first wife was the daughter of a Cleveland industrialist, and she lived with Dahlberg for a brief period in Paris and in Brussels. Absorbed by his work on the novel, he had little time to devote to his marriage: in addition, his wife suspected that he had married her solely for her inheritance, and they drifted apart until she finally deserted him in Brussels, where Dahlberg finished writing the novel. Arabella York, the wife of Richard Aldington, sent the manuscript of *Bottom Dogs* to D. H. Lawrence in Bandol, and Lawrence agreed to write a preface to the book. As Harold Billings notes, Lawrence's introduction was a somewhat mixed blessing in terms of Dahlberg's subsequent literary career because it characterizes Dahlberg as a Naturalist par excellence; and "now any criticism of Dahlberg's work begins and ends with his statement." [8] According to Walter Lowenfels, Dahlberg, furious about Lawrence's comments, wrote him angry letters expressing his disagreement with Lawrence's interpretation of the novel.[9] Dahlberg describes his own reaction to Lawrence's preface in *The Confessions.*

*Bottom Dogs* received somewhat mixed reviews, most reviewers taking their cue from Lawrence's preface. With the publication of *From Flushing to Calvary* in 1932, Dahlberg's literary image became fixed as a hard-line proletarian Naturalist who emphasized the sordid and decadent aspects of American life. His next book, *Those Who Perish,* derived from his experiences traveling in Germany in 1933. Shaken and embittered by the increasing inroads of fascism, Dahlberg became politically active for the first time in his life and became a frequent contributor to *New Masses, The Nation,* and *The New Republic.* In 1935, he was an organizer of the Marxist-oriented American Writer's Congress, and he delivered a remarkable paper on "Fascism and Writers" to the first meeting of the congress in that year.

Dahlberg abandoned an attempt at a third autobiographical novel, a portion of which was published in *Signature* magazine in the spring of 1936. In *The Forum,* published in the fall of the following year, Ford Madox Ford named William Carlos Williams, E. E. Cummings, and Edward Dahlberg as the three most neglected writers in America. (Somewhat ironically, *Book World,* some three decades later in its June 2, 1968, issue, headed its list of "Ten neglected American writers who deserve to be better known" with the name of Edward Dahlberg.

In the late 1930's, Dahlberg and Dorothy Norman started a literary magazine of their own entitled *Twice a Year.* The association was short-lived, however, as Dahlberg had a disagreement with his co-editor regarding a manuscript submitted by Ford Madox Ford. When she refused to pay Ford for an article they had commissioned about Stephen Crane, Dahlberg withdrew from the magazine after working on only the first issue. At the suggestion of Ford, Dahlberg helped organize a group of writers called the "Friends of William Carlos Williams" whose aim it was to give Williams's work a wider audience. Included in the group were Sherwood Anderson, Paul Rosenfeld, Marsden Hartley, and Alfred Stieglitz. The group met regularly at the Downtown Gallery on Thirteenth Street in New York City and sponsored various literary events.

In the early 1940's Dahlberg traveled widely throughout the United States and Mexico. Disheartened by the meager reception given the publication of his iconoclastic critical work, *Do These Bones Live,* he "dropped into the pit of Acheron, a long oblivion," [10] as he writes in a letter to Robert Hutchins. In 1942 he married Winifred Sheehan Moore[11] who gave birth to his two sons, Geoffrey and Joel. He spent a great deal of his time caring for his aging mother, and his correspondence during these years reflects his increasing bitterness. A revision of his critical work appeared in London in 1947 with a preface by Sir Herbert Read celebrating the book as one of the most remarkable prose works of our time. But Read's words evidently had little impact, for Dahlberg's next book, *The Flea of Sodom,* attracted even less attention. It was reviewed in only three periodicals, including a rather severe condemnation in *Poetry* accusing Dahlberg of Fascist tendencies.[12]

After another marriage, this time to R'lene LaFleur Howell, Dahlberg lived variously in New York and California, contributed regularly to the little magazines, and often appeared in the *New Directions Annual.* Deeply engrossed in Pre-Columbian American history, he began work on *The Sorrows of Priapus,* a book which he describes in a letter to Lewis Mumford as "a little book on whether man should have a phallus or not." [13] Sir Herbert Read suggested that Dahlberg send the manuscript of *The Sorrows* to James Laughlin at New Directions; Laughlin agreed to publish part of it in a handsome edition illustrated by Ben Shahn. Read again wrote a preface for the book, and Dahlberg's work began raising a few eyebrows when it appeared in 1957.

In the early 1950's Dahlberg lived in Santa Monica, California, and then in New York. His correspondence of this period laments the difficulty he had finding a publisher although his work had been admired by many important literary figures. An indefatigable correspondent, he suggested to Sir Herbert Read that they undertake an epistolary exchange about modern letters; and he proposed the title "The New Dunciad" for the collection. Read agreed to the exchange, and the work was published under the title of *Truth Is More Sacred,* which is taken from a quotation Dahlberg cites from Socrates. Again, the work had little impact, although Dahlberg became publicly associated with Read as a kind of literary elder statesman.

In 1956, Dahlberg departed for Europe for another long stay abroad to begin extensive work on his autobiography, *Because I Was Flesh.* He returned to New York for a brief period and then spent four years in Mallorca, living in a stone house by the sea and working on the autobiography. During this period, he received a grant from the Longview Foundation and from the National Institute of Arts and Letters to enable him to complete this work. In 1964, *Because I was Flesh* appeared and received wide acclaim. As I have mentioned, the work was nominated for the National Book Award of that year, and Dahlberg was heralded as a major American prose stylist. Recognition was coming slowly, but unquestionably it was coming.

In 1965, he returned from Mallorca after a brief stay in Dublin, and he accepted a position as a visiting professor at the University of Missouri in his native Kansas City. In the same year, *Reasons of the Heart,* a collection of aphorisms, was published, and he received another grant, this time from the Rockefeller Foundation. The following year saw the publication of his collected poems, *Cinpango's Hinder Door,* by the University of Texas Press, with an introduction by Allen Tate. In 1967, the Dahlberg "renaissance" culminated with the publication of much previously uncollected material. An *Edward Dahlberg Reader* containing excerpts from Dahlberg's non-novelistic works and several letters was edited by Paul Carroll for New Directions. George Braziller issued a selection of Dahlberg's letters entitled *Epitaphs of Our Time,* and Roger Beacham Publishers collected several previously unpublished essays and poems in a slim volume called *The Leafless American.* The following year, 1968, the "other half" of *The Sorrows of Priapus* was published as *The Carnal Myth;* shortly after its appearance, Dahlberg left for Europe to live in Dublin and Rome. He returned to the United States in the summer of 1968 to reside in New York and to work on a sequel to *Because I Was Flesh, The Confessions of Edward Dahlberg,* which retells the story of his life in allegorical fashion and which was published by Braziller in 1971.

## II *The Evolution of a Style*

More than the work of most writers, Dahlberg's literary development needs to be considered in its entirety in order for us to assess his accomplishments and to evaluate his proper place in the history of American letters. But assessing the totality of Dahlberg's work presents several problems since we are dealing with the work of a living writer whose most creative work may be yet before him. If the work of the past five or six years is any indication, we can hardly ignore the possibility that Dahlberg's most productive years are still to come. On the other hand, we have enough of the work to begin laying the groundwork for judgment, and a study of the development of Dahlberg's literary career tells us a great deal about the "education" of an important and influential American writer and about the "ripening" of his prose style.

Hassan has noted that Dahlberg's books reveal "the evolution of a style, the transformation of a man." [14] The evolution has been from Naturalism to Classicism; the transformation, from Marxism to humanism. These isms, of course, are simply convenient terms which can serve only as broad labels with which to characterize certain tendencies at various stages of Dahlberg's development. Although the Marxist inclinations of *Those Who Perish* become suspect in the later works, the broad humanistic base of his thought is already evident in the "proletarian period," which, as I have already suggested, was hardly proletarian in the traditional sense of the word. The 1930's were what Dahlberg calls his "literary apprenticeship," and he was already engaged in a project of self-education that was to shape and direct his future work.

The Classical basis of that education can be garnered from advice offered to other writers in Dahlberg's letters. In a letter to Isabella Gardner, the contemporary poet, Dahlberg writes: "What I want to say to you is very simple: shun modern books. Go back to Beginnings: ritual will heal a line, a stanza, your whole head; you need symbols, Isis, Hathor, Typhon, the Kabala for your image and vision. Go to school with some Master, Ovid, Plutarch, Livy, Tacitus, and you will then find the river back to your own identity."[15] In response to Miss Gardner's request for a reading list, Dahlberg recommends the following books:

1. First volume of Strabo in the Loeb Library of Classics
2. First volume of Diodorus of Siculus in Loeb
3. Complete Poems of Christopher Smart
4. Works of Herodotus
5. William Gilchrist's *Life of William Blake*
6. Coleridge's *Biographia Literaria*
7. Harrison's *Prolegomena to the Study of Greek Religion*
8. Navarette's edition of *Columbus' Four Voyages*
9. de la Vega's *The History of Florida*
10. Harrison's *Themis*
11. Suetonius' *Twelve Caesars* trans. by Philomen Holland
12. Barcia's *Chronicles* trans. by A. Kerrigan[16]

In the continuing "battle of the books" between ancients and moderns, it is quite clear on which side Dahlberg stands. The important thing to note, however, is that he regards the major function of these books to be their ability to shape the style of prose and poetry by infusing it with image, symbol, and ritual which have a universal bearing. As he asserts in the letter to Miss Gardner, they enable us to "find the river back to [our] own identity."

## III *Literary Critic*

When we have become cognizant of Dahlberg's preference for the literature of the past, we are hardly surprised to discover that his opinions of contemporary writers contrast with the critical temper of his time. Indeed, this fact probably more than any other makes Dahlberg seem "distant" to us, out of touch with the main literary currents of the day. His evaluations of other writers, some of whom are among the "sacred cows" of our academies, often strike us as arrogant, eccentric, and unresponsive to the major literary achievements of our age. In *Truth Is More Sacred*, an exchange of letters between Dahlberg and Sir Herbert Read, he attacks James Joyce, Lawrence, Pound, Eliot, and Robert Graves. In *Alms for Oblivion*, he calls F. Scott Fitzgerald's work "peopleless fiction" and deems even Herman Melville's *Moby Dick* an "epical failure." What are we to make of this high priest of the literary art who so consistently disparages the literary worth of his contemporaries and some of the most innovative works of English and American letters?

The answer is, of course, that we should examine his critical approach and try to understand the foundations of his attack before dismissing his opinions as eccentric. For, despite the fact that he often overstates his case, Dahlberg's critical remarks give us reason to question our traditional evaluations and to re-examine our conditioned attitude toward the major literary figures of our time. Literature, he seems to be telling us, must help us to understand ourselves. The moment writers begin to substitute literary concerns for human problems, their writing becomes sterile and superfluous. A great writer must be a great man, and the two identities are inseparable. He is more concerned with the fact that Ernest Hemingway and William Faulkner, for example, never adequately expressed their gratitude to Sherwood Anderson for his literary assistance than he is with their contributions to the novel:

> Hemingway was a boorish and uncultivated man, and he was a disciple of Sherwood Anderson from whom he learned little or nothing, and whom he lampooned in *The Torrents of Spring*. So was Faulkner a disciple of Anderson's. Neither one, it is forlorn to relate, ever showed their gratitude to their master. The master was human, warm, and good; the disciples were eviscerated, without feeling, void of that sorrow which pervades all great literature. All we look for in order to understand ourselves is absent in the books of Faulkner and Hemingway.[17]

The same equation between a man's life and his work is evident in the comments in his letters about various other literary figures. Speaking of Richard Eberhart, he writes to Josephine Herbst: "The truth is I do not know whether he is a good poet or not. Since he did not reply to [my letter] I suspect he is not." [18]

Whether Dahlberg is motivated by malevolence or moralism is often difficult to decide. In either case, Dahlberg's *ad hominem* approach to these writers—his preoccupation with biographical, moral, or historical concerns at the expense of critical analysis—is clearly at odds with the main tenor of twentieth-century literary criticism. We can easily understand why an esthetically oriented critic would bristle at the suggestion that a poet's work may be judged by whether or not he answers his mail. We might consider, however, that the great tradition of English literary criticism which comes to us from Sir Philip Sidney, Samuel Johnson, Matthew Arnold, and others, has always been essentially moralistic; and it is not surprising that Dahlberg takes these men for his mentors rather than René Wellek and Austin Warren. In this context, we should not be too quick to condemn a writer whose primary concerns are moral rather than esthetic, and who sees literature as functional rather than decorative.

It remains somewhat ironic that a writer whom Alfred Kazin in 1942 called "exhausted by his own sensibilities" [19] should emerge in the 1960's as a kind of elder statesman of American letters. The first really serious consideration of Dahlberg's work did not occur until 1947 with the publication of Herbert Read's preface to *Sing O Barren.* At that time, Dahlberg had already been writing for almost twenty years with scant critical recognition. He is still represented in the anthologies as a proletarian writer, but recently the later work has aroused interest and acclaim. A very different judgment comes from Kazin in 1964 when he writes that the final pages of *Because I Was Flesh* "attain a beauty of truthfulness beyond anything I have read in recent American writings." [20] Clearly, the apex of Dahlberg's achievement comes rather late in life, and it is appropriate that his literary reputation should grow as the author of *Because I Was Flesh* and *The Sorrows of Priapus,* rather than as the man who penned *Bottom Dogs* and *Those Who Perish.*

A look at Dahlberg's earlier work does, however, shed a great deal of light on his later development, for the carefully structured, richly allusive sentences of *Because I Was Flesh* assume an additional luster when placed beside the spare, Naturalistic passages of *Bottom Dogs* which deal with the same subject but which lack the thirty-five years of stylistic development that inform the later work. It is for this reason, rather than the simply chronological arrangement, that any study of Dahlberg must begin with his proletarian period if it is to account for the mature literary mind that emerges in the 1960's to produce one of our most distinctive prose stylists.

CHAPTER 2

# The Humanist as Naturalist

THE term "proletarian novel" has always seemed to me, despite my use of it, a somewhat inaccurate one with which to describe Edward Dahlberg's early novels. Since they were written in the depression years and deal with lower-class life in America, it is a convenient label; but, when we examine the works in more detail, we find it misleading. If we think of a proletarian novel in Walter Rideout's terms as simply a novel "written by a member of the working class about, presumably, working class characters," [1] the term may be generally applicable. But the phrase connotes more often a work of fiction imbued with the dogmatics of a Marxist ideology which attempts to inform its readers of the dynamics of the class struggle and to enlist their support in behalf of the working classes. In this sense, *Bottom Dogs* and *From Flushing to Calvary* fail to meet the requirements of the genre. Both are bleak, despairing books in the Naturalistic mode; but they are hardly aimed at inspiring the workers of the world to unite.

## I Bottom Dogs

In the October 25, 1932, issue of *Contempo* magazine, Dahlberg remarks about *Bottom Dogs:* "Now in order to please the Communists I might have had Lorry dash up to the *New Masses* offices or elsewhere and ask for membership in the Party. But then I would no longer be a novelist but a liar. For this would no more be possible for Lorry than for that other pathetic American protagonist in Dreiser's *An American Tragedy.*" [2]

Even more to the point, Lorry Lewis, the central character of *Bottom Dogs,* explicitly rejects Marxism in the latter pages of the novel: "He didn't know whether the country owed him a living; he didn't go in much for politics or socialism, whatever they called it. He had read some of Jack London a little, once tried 'The

Dream of Debs,' but didn't quite get it."[3] Despite the coolness to Marxist aims and methods, *Bottom Dogs* was an influential novel in the 1930's and 1940's which spawned a host of "street gamin" novels, as Dahlberg calls them; and it added the term "bottom dog novel" to our literary jargon. James T. Farrell's *Studs Lonigan Trilogy,* Henry Roth's *Call It Sleep,* and Willard Motley's *Knock on Any Door* are examples of the genre, and they may serve to suggest the degree and scope of the novel's impact on the American fiction of the two decades which followed it.

"Many men write books," says Dahlberg, quoting Tolstoi in a preface to a new edition of *Bottom Dogs* published in 1961, "but few are ashamed of them afterward" (iii). It is not surprising that the author of *The Sorrows of Priapus* should look back at his apprentice work with such disdain. However, it does seem a mistake to dismiss the novel as inconsequential not only because of its influence on later American fiction but also because it provides us with a frank and unsparing "portrait of the artist as a young man" with a distinctly American consciousness of time and place.

The central plot line of *Bottom Dogs* is quite simple. Episodic in structure, the novel relates the story of Lorry Lewis, his childhood in Kansas City, the trials and tribulations of his mother Lizzie after her desertion by Lorry's father, Lorry's experiences in a Cleveland orphanage, and finally his drifting about the country in search of a sense of purpose. The novel's debt to Theodore Dreiser's *An American Tragedy* seems apparent. Like the Dreiserian classic, it is a novel of initiation that stresses the environmental forces which shape the central character's needs and motivations. Lorry and Clyde Griffiths are indeed literary brothers —both are the product of broken homes and are denied participation in the promise of American life. In the Naturalistic tradition, the lives of the characters in *Bottom Dogs* are described in the bleakest of terms, and the animalistic struggle for existence is paramount. In the often quoted brief introduction to the first edition of the novel, D. H. Lawrence notes: "Those boys [in the orphanage] are much less than animals. They are cold wills functioning with a minimum of consciousness. . . . They are brutally and deliberately unaware" (xiv).

A sense of aimlessness and drift permeates the novel from its opening pages. The very first sentence contrasts the quest for purpose and stability which dominates Lorry's mother's life with the hard facts of her vagabond existence: "She moved from town to town, selling hair switches, giving osteopathic treatments, going on again when she felt the place had been played out. In this way she hoped to save a little money and establish herself in some thriving city" (1). But Lizzie never realizes her dream, and the stability she seeks remains beyond her grasp. The prosperous times of "Teddy Roosevelt Days" (as the first chapter is entitled) seem destined to benefit other people, but the prosperity makes little impact upon the lives of Lorry and his mother.

Lizzie Lewis, however, is not given to complaining; indeed, the most persistent fact about her is her dedication to a life of struggle and hard times. As if to compensate for the inherent emptiness of her life, she never veers from her determined course to seek a new marriage partner and to provide sustenance for Lorry. When the two aims conflict, however, she sends Lorry to an orphanage in hopes of being in a better position to marry. Though the exigencies of her situation demand that she send Lorry away, Lizzie remains intensely concerned about the welfare of her son. She pursues her vocation as a lady barber in order to earn enough money to be self-sufficient, but she is always disturbed about the insufficient amount of time she is able to devote to Lorry as a mother. One of the novel's central ironies is that this well-intentioned woman must abandon her son in an orphanage in order to make it possible for her to seek a better life for him. As Lizzie tells one of the girl barbers she works with, "it's no disgrace to be poor, but it's awfully unconvenient" (26).

The decision to send Lorry to the orphanage is instigated by one of Lizzie's suitors, Henry Smith, the captain of a Missouri River excursion boat. In sharp contrast to Lizzie's strong feelings about sending her son away, Henry's thoughts on the matter are callous and selfish. After Lorry is sent away, "Henry felt relieved. The kid probably would be out of the way at least for three or four years" (40). It seems clear that Dahlberg wishes to exonerate Lizzie from any failure of parental responsibility for what occurs to Lorry during his long hours and days at the orphanage.

The grim, Spartan quality of life in the Cleveland asylum is described in the most Naturalistic terms, which emphasize the depravity and degradation that the orphans had to face:

> The orphans were called by rows to the washroom in which there was a long, narrow trough on either side with some twenty faucets which shot ice cold water into the cement bottom. There were rectangular cakes of Ivory soap in each plate and numbered toothbrushes adjacent to them. The kids filed in, their young bodies stripped to the waist, the sleeves of their woolen underwear hanging, and splashed their faces, necks, ears, and hands in an ice cold douche that came out swift as water from a fire pump. Then they dug the bristles of their toothbrushes into the Ivory cakes and scrubbed their teeth. (45)

This quality of the novel surely led Lawrence to conclude his introduction on an ambivalent note: "I don't want to read any more books like this. But I am glad to have read this one, just to know what is the last word in repulsive consciousness, consciousness in a state of repulsion" (xvi-xvii). It is indeed difficult to take *Bottom Dogs* in large doses because of its unsparing portrait of life under minimal *human* conditions.

The events of Lorry's life in the orphanage are narrated in terms of his relationships to the other orphans, two of whom are characterized in great detail. Two entire chapters are devoted to Herman Mush Tate and Bonehead-Star-Wolfe, and they emerge, apart from Lorry and his mother, as the most memorable characters in the novel. Dahlberg's gift for characterization is developed in these two sketches, and they anticipate his masterful portrayal of Tobias Emeritch, one of Lizzie's suitors in *Because I Was Flesh.* His technique is to make use of selected details which imply a great deal about a character without being overly explicit about it. We learn, for example, of Herman Mush Tate's cowardice, braggadocio, and vanity in the following brief, economical passage: "Herman Mush Tate was always hanging around after fights were over, looking for battlefield souvenirs, agates that fell out of a guy's pocket when he was taking an honest-to-god swing at a mick, and later he would talk himself up, boasting how he had stepped on the necks of three micks himself" (73).

The fact that Bonehead-Star-Wolfe is an outsider in the orphanage and disliked by most of the orphans is suggested by this description: "On Wednesday evenings, when they got biscuits with raisins in them, Bonehead-Star-Wolfe would slowly and agonizingly nibble away at his biscuit long after all the rest of the kids had finished theirs. Even Mugsy, who used to watch him from the other table, said it wasn't human" (107–8). Another orphan, Prunes, finally becomes the only one who befriends Bonehead-Star-Wolfe, and a note of pathos is introduced when we learn that Bonehead later dies in a Denver sanitorium for consumptives and that Prunes is killed in World War I. These two chapters, through the use of carefully selected details, give us a sense of closeness with the characters involved and unfold a continuing human drama through the presentation of projected events in the characters' lives.

After Lorry's release from the orphanage, he lives for a while in "the nigger section of Cleveland" with two classmates. He begins questioning the purposelessness of his life and yearns to return to Kansas City in search of something more meaningful. At this point in Lorry's young life, Kansas City represents a kind of paradise lost in contrast to the sterility of the orphanage and to the bleakness of Cleveland's "Cedar Avenue Nights." In Kansas City, "There were the horse stables, the stockyards, the 12th Street blues, the old timers; Muriel was there, and other grown-up gals, whom he knew as a kid" (126). The fact that Lorry glorifies his Kansas City past is tempered by his realization that things will have changed, and he is particularly worried about seeing his mother again after so many years have passed.

Like Paul Morel in *Sons and Lovers,* he resents the fact that his mother will have aged, that the energy and vitality he associates with her will have given way to the immobility and drabness of old age. The relationship between Lorry Lewis and his mother has much in common with the relationship between Paul and Gertrude Morel in the Lawrence novel. While the underlying sexual attraction of the mother is much less explicit in Dahlberg's work, it is surely something of a latent Oedipal attachment that Lorry feels in much of *Bottom Dogs*. The following dialogue between Paul Morel and his mother from *Sons and Lovers* has, though less direct, a counterpart in *Bottom Dogs:*

> "Why can't a man have a *young* mother? What is she old for?"
> "Well," his mother laughed, "she can scarcely help it."
> ". . . What are you old for!" he said, mad with his impotence. "*Why* can't you come with me to places?"
> "At one time," she replied, "I could have run up that hill a good deal better than you."

"What's the good of that to *me?*" he cried, hitting his fist on the wall.[4]

We have no such direct confrontation in *Bottom Dogs,* but Lorry's thoughts at the end of Chapter VI strike much the same chord. He has finally decided to return to Kansas City, but the worry of confronting his mother once more begins to gnaw at him: "He was afraid she was getting old-looking, with signs of aging decay about her face and mouth and hair. That always troubled him, his mother decaying under work, her flesh drying up as the years peeled off the fresh skin over her cheeks, leaving something taut and old like a canvas tent pushed in by a rainstorm. That bothered him, and he was afraid for a little to go back" (127).

Lorry's anxiety about his mother's aging is also related to his growing fear about his return to Kansas City. For, in reality, the Kansas City to which he returns is not the idealistic vision he has conjured; it is as grim and dirty as Cleveland and as inhospitable as the orphanage. All of these changes are personified in his mother's aging and even more particularly in the condition of her place of business, the Star Ladies Barber Shop. Dahlberg spares us no Naturalistic detail in his description of Lorry's first impression of the place upon returning: "Lorry went into the back of the shop. The old, rusty gas range was still there; on it were some round black pots, the sides of some bent in; the toilet water was running; it never did flush right, his mother used to say. A roach crawled across the fly-speckled, white plaster. On the table was a bit of frayed, greasy oilcloth, a loaf cut jaggedly, partly by knife, on the other parts thumb and finger depressions could be seen" (131). Much like the young man in Joyce's "Araby," Lorry is disillusioned by a confrontation with the reality of the ideal he has been constructing in his mind—an ideal totally out of touch with things as they actually are and one based solely on romantic notions and unrealistic hopes.

The next few chapters of the novel describe Lorry's brief stay in Kansas City, but they focus more particularly on Lizzie Lewis and her continuing courtships. Lorry's mother may be aging, but she has not abandoned her pursuit of a husband. There is both humor and pathos in her "affairs" with Harry Coen, the owner of a "high class" bakery in Kansas City, and in the return of Henry Smith, one of Lizzie's most persistent suitors who never quite fulfills her idea of what a husband should be. Finally rejecting Smith for the last time, Lizzie experiences a sense of nostalgia and regret, and she momentarily realizes that her quest for a suitable marriage partner is a futile one indeed. Staring at the lace curtains in her living room "which flagged back and forth against the September breeze," she reminds one briefly of Katherine Mansfield's Miss Brill whose illusions of life's potential fall by the wayside as she becomes cognizant for the first time of herself as others see her.

In the novel's final five chapters, Lorry again moves to the center of the work, thereby replacing his mother as the dominant character. Chapter X, entitled "Ridin' the Blinds," begins with Lorry's thinking about leaving Kansas City, again in search of purpose and adventure. As always, luck and fortune are just around the corner, or so he imagines, if only he can be free of his present dilemma. He has visions of becoming a salesman so that he can "wear classy vests, and wind up seeing the Grand Canyon" (176). But Lorry is uncertain about his sales abilities—he feels he lacks the "backbone" necessary for successful salesmanship. In desperation, he takes a job as a magazine subscription salesman—"The word salesman was avoided; they were not salesmen, they were told, but educators" (178)—in Beatrice, Nebraska. His experience in Beatrice, going from door to door reciting a bland and trumped-up sales pitch, verifies his suspicion that salesmanship is not one of his talents. Every time he repeats the pitch his mind wanders to that "westbound train," and the lure of the road proves stronger than that of the dollar.

Lorry runs out on the job and moves on to Omaha, but here too he almost immediately feels the need to leave. Like Kansas City and Cleveland, Omaha offers little promise and excitement. Dahlberg continually emphasizes Lorry's sense of transience and impermanence—his impatience with a stationary, immobile life: "he had to get out of Omaha; couldn't stand sticking around there anymore; he was fed up with it" (185). Greening, Wyoming, Ogden, Utah, Salt Lake City—which appear to Lorry the grim, dessicated towns of America's heartland—pass one by one; and, as each seems a carbon copy of the next, each reactivates his urge to get back on the road.

Initially, San Francisco seems to be the promised land Lorry has been seeking. His initial impression of the city is described in almost poetic terms—at least poetic in comparison to the unadorned prose of the earlier part of the novel. "He liked Frisco, he wished he could live there: San Francisco was a Scotchmist light tweed topcoat on his back . . . the windy Chicago of the coast, a grey *Times* flapping up against the curb blued by late autumn" (213). But shortly he realizes that the glamor and glitter of the California city is all façade, "tricked up for the tourist and the Iowans by the sea as the Californians spotted them" (214). A brief encounter with a homosexual heightens the growing feeling of revulsion in Lorry, and we find him next in Los Angeles, still in search of a substantive life.

Lorry's experiences in Los Angeles are more satisfying and enjoyable to him than any previously described in the novel. He moves into the YMCA and becomes good friends with Max Maxwell, a kind of good-natured hustler who takes pride in swindling swindlers. Max and his friends are more knowledgeable and worldly than any of Lorry's previous associates on the road or in other towns in which he has lived. Their hedonistic outlook on life teaches Lorry to enjoy living in the present and to stop worrying about the uncertainties of his future. Though only a momentary respite from the desperation of his life on the road, Lorry's stay at the "Y" is full of good times and fun. The "After Bible Coffee Class" turns into a happy poker party which eventually proves too much for Herbert Hibbens, the stern social secretary of the organization, to endure. When Max, wielding a toilet plunger, chases Lorry out of the shower and forces him to run naked into the hallway, Lorry is asked to pack up and leave.

The final chapter finds Lorry at Solomon's Dancepalace in Los Angeles, which is described in terms of an unreality not characteristic of most of the novel's descriptive material. This artificial world of colored lights and Japanese lanterns sharply contrasts to the sparse black and white quality of the orphanage or to the drabness of America's midwestern cities. In this world that offers temporary escape from the monotonous sameness of everyday life, Lorry can again forget for a moment his purposeless existence and pursue the pleasures of the flesh. But the artificial lighting which dominates Dahlberg's description of the dance palace is symbolic of the artificiality of the situation. Lorry is "pale, sick looking under the jaundiced electric lights" (260) which distort true perspective and prevent him from seeing clearly. After a disappointing sexual experience with a girl whom he picks up at Solomon's, Lorry again ruminates about the future of his life, and the novel ends on the note of drift and aimlessness that has characterized it from the beginning:

> Perhaps, he would go east, get out of it all, he could run away; but he couldn't go side-door Pullman again, that was finished. Boing, sleeping in coal cars, riding those railroad broncos, going to strange hotel rooms, the ghastly plaster inside those empty clothesclosets, walking the streets—all that was done, but then, how did he know? Anyhow, if he got the clap he would go to the Los Angeles City hospital; maybe, those enamelled iron beds, the white sheets, the medical immaculateness of it all, might do something to him. Something had to happen; and he knew nothing would. . . . (268–69)

Having gone as far west as he could go, Lorry speculates about returning to the East, but with the speculation comes the realization that there is really nowhere to turn, nowhere to escape the frustrating uneventfulness of his life; and even the sterile image of the hospital seems more hopeful than the life he has to anticipate. Recently Dahlberg has often remarked that the only reason we travel is because there is no place to go, and this observation certainly applies to Lorry Lewis. For Lorry, life without purpose or meaning is no life at all, and *Bottom Dogs* is essentially a search for meaning which ends without discovering any. In Dahlberg's later works, he discovers meaning in man's awareness of his cultural heritage, in the universality of myth, and on the continuity of the human condition. But in *Bottom Dogs* he writes as a Naturalist who sees life as determined by environment and man as a prisoner of random and uncertain forces which he is powerless to control.

## II From Flushing to Calvary

Lorry Lewis's story is continued in *From Flushing to Calvary* which appeared in 1932, three years after *Bottom Dogs.* Dahlberg's second novel focuses more intently on the life of Lizzie Lewis than does its predecessor, and she emerges as the novel's central character. The book opens with Lorry and his mother reunited and living in Bensonhurst, New York. Through a series of flashbacks and interior monologues, we learn of the events that have transpired in Lorry's life since the conclusion of *Bottom Dogs*. We discover that Max Maxwell has given Lorry three hundred dollars in order to help him return to Kansas City to begin a new start in life. In Kansas City, he convinces his mother to sell the Star Ladies Barber Shop and to move to New York in search of a better life. In New York, he and his mother first live in an "ashen stucco house" in Bensonhurst and then move into two rooms and a kitchen in a three-story tenement opposite Calvary Cemetery in Queens.

Several recurrent notes run through the novel. The most humorous aspects come from Lizzie's never-ending quest for a husband ("She told Lorry that she was answering these marriage ads more for the excitement of it than anything else.")[5] and from her remarkable moneymaking schemes, most notably her "cure" for pregnancy, which wins her one customer after another. Probably the funniest episode in the novel occurs when Dahlberg brings together Lizzie's two main concerns and has one of her most serious suitors, a prudish, solemn miser named Hervey, discover Lizzie in the act of administering one of her cures:

> Then he just had to look. Stooping down, he slowly picked the key out of the lock, tiptoed over to a shaky spindly table and put it down. Then he came back and peeked through. The buzzing had stopped. Mrs. Schroeder was lying on her back, her legs up, her dress back, like an awning loosely drawn up. Lizzie was working on her. Her chugging and bustling, the female words that passed between them, made Hervey's head drip with perspiration. His eyes steamed. Finally, he couldn't stand it any longer. He was so exhausted he had to sink into Willie's canvas-cot. (149–50)

Lizzie shortly reveals to Hervey her avocation, particularly the wonders of the violet-ray machine that she uses to cure most illnesses. Fascinated by this information, Hervey asks Lizzie if she can help him with pains he has in the back of the neck, and he also requests a scalp treatment.

Though there is much that is humorous in *From Flushing to Calvary*, it is ultimately a quite serious novel which laments the essential desperation of Lizzie Lewis's life even to a greater degree than *Bottom Dogs*. The major theme of the novel is the impending death of Lorry's mother, and throughout the work Dahlberg's descriptive setting reinforces this theme. The cold, barren "wasteland" background that is the keynote of the descriptive passages emphasizes the emptiness and lack of fulfillment in Lizzie's life. The rows of ashen stucco houses, "shaped like Camel cigarette boxes" (3), are as dull and dreary as the lives of those who inhabit them. "The materials of which they are composed," Dahlberg writes, "are dirt cheap. They are job-lot houses" (3).

Again, this type of description of the lives of America's lower classes would seem to place Dahlberg in the proletarian tradition, but again Marxist dogmatics are conspicuously absent. At one point in the novel, Lorry, who has become a voracious reader, does try to familiarize himself with the main tenets of Marxism; but the idea of class consciousness remains to him simply an abstract concept that has no clear relationship to his own life: "he recalled a book he had picked up at a secondhand bookstore. The author, whom he had never heard of before, was a man named Trotsky. Lorry had never paid much attention to politics. He had never been able to see where it let him in" (85–86). After reading the book, Lorry experiences no revelatory conversion, as does, for example, Jack London's Martin Eden; instead, he continues the methodical sameness of his life. Lorry's story might easily be interpreted, in fact, as an implicit rejection of Marxism as the ultimate hope for America's masses.

Structurally and stylistically, *From Flushing to Calvary* is a more sophisticated work than its predecessor. The fragmented chronological sequence of the narrative is in keeping with the literary experimentation of the day—and it is worth noting that Faulkner's *The Sound and the Fury* was published in 1929, the same year that *Bottom Dogs* appeared in England. The first forty-five pages of *From Flushing to Calvary* move in direct chronological order; then there is an extended flashback which covers some of the same ground as *Bottom Dogs* and relates Lizzie's earlier experiences in Kansas City. This flashback continues through page 69 where the narrative returns to Lizzie's present life in Bensonhurst. On page 70 Lorry moves to the center of the work, and we learn of his adventures in Los Angeles after *Bottom Dogs,* and of his decision to return to Kansas City in order to take his mother to New York and "settle down." Part II of the novel begins with Lorry and his mother having moved from Bensonhurst to Calvary and is narrated in simple chronological sequence. Part III, entitled "Daily Graphic Slabs," chronicles in detail the inner state of Lizzie's mind and her absorption with death. The use of newspaper headlines from obituary columns suggests the influence of John Dos Passos, as does the interior-monologue technique in Part IV, which is somewhat analogous to the "camera-eye" sections of *U.S.A.* In this section, the inner conflicts of Lorry's consciousness are explored. Part V relates Lorry's decision to leave his mother and return for a visit to the Cleveland orphan asylum in which he had grown up. This experience triggers a Proustian flood of memories about his youthful life and parallels the orphanage chapters in *Bottom Dogs.* The novel's final section (later published separately as *Kentucky Blue Grass Henry Smith*) deals with Lorry's return to New York; with his mother's final reverie recalling her courtship with Henry Smith, her most romantic suitor; and with her death while undergoing an operation for an intestinal growth.

The disjointed chronological structure of *From Flushing to Calvary* gives the novel a psychological dimension absent in *Bottom Dogs,* and it also indicates Dahlberg's awareness of the major literary currents of his day. I am not suggesting that the work illustrates the use of interior monologue as subtley and effectively as *The Sound and the Fury,* nor that Dahlberg has mastered the psychological narrative to the degree of a James Joyce or a Virginia Woolf. However, this additional dimension of *From Flushing to Calvary* reveals a movement away from the journalistic Naturalism that was the major mode of *Bottom Dogs,* and it also foreshadows Dahlberg's impatience with the limitations of the Naturalistic method. "I began as a naturalist," he states in an interview, "and I discovered that employing the vernacular was not very effective; that uncouth words were not a path toward the inward nature of man." [6] While the vernacular is not entirely abandoned in *From Flushing to Calvary,* it is used more sparingly; moreover, it is tempered by a metaphoric and allusive prose that was to become the hallmark of his later style.

This metaphoric style is perhaps best epitomized in the "Daily Graphic Slabs" section of the novel in which Lorry has a dream that brings together several of the book's secondary themes. Having left his mother on her sickbed, Lorry has a nightmare in which all of the images he associates with her sick, tortuous life make an indelible impression upon him. The transience of his life, the artificiality of his escape, his alienation from a meaningful past, and the final permanence of death are all brought home to him clearly in the imagery of the nightmare:

> He had started up out of a bad dream, a dream stuffed with ratty secondhand furs, holey shoes, red-blooded suitcases lying in the showwindow of a 14th Street pawnshop. There were trapdrum moons, bassdrum streetlamps, gilded grapefruit pawnshop balls, all lit up by diamond electric lights.
>
> Out of that he had suddenly come into a room full of mahogany furniture; it had the slick mahogany finish of Calvary hearses. Then he was stopped short by a woman who pointed to a skinny toothpick heap underneath a white sheet on a brassy saxaphone bed. He knew it was his mother. The tears ran down his cheeks. He ran to her and knelt down and petted and fondled her; then he tickled her underneath the chin, as if with a dandelion, and asked her whether she liked butter. He tried to get nearer and nearer to her. And when he couldn't reach her, and he couldn't mix his warm breath with hers, for she didn't have any, not even a cigarette wisp of breath, for she was a dead oilswamp sea, he wept more and more, as if his heart, stone-still, had been touched by a mosaic rod. The tears, sweet-sour and bitter in his mouth, were a passover bitterness. (201)

This remarkable dream demonstrates Dahlberg's ability, at this early stage in his career, to use symbols and imagery effectively and concisely. The ratty furs, the holey shoes, and the red-blooded suitcases are symbolic of a violent and depraved past which Lorry has attempted to put behind him and out of his mind. His attempt at repression is unsuccessful, however, as the objects are ironically in the window of a pawnshop waiting to be claimed. The artificial lights and gilded pawnshop balls are appropriate symbols for the artificiality of his escape. The polished mahogany furniture recalling Calvary hearses, indicative of the permanence and irrevocability of death, appear, just before the actuality of his mother's death, which is imaged as a totally inanimate "skinny toothpick heap underneath a white sheet." Lorry attempts to retrieve and re-create his past by achieving a bond with his mother that he had been unable to achieve in life; but, of course, the attempt is futile, and he weeps in repentance.

If the theme of death culminates in the "Daily Graphic Slabs" section of the novel, the theme of artificiality reaches its apex in the section entitled "Coney Island Angelus Bells." This episode opens with Lorry's turning to religion for the first time to seek some solace for his troubled life. But the attempt is short-lived; some friends of his arrive and remind him that he has promised to attend "mardi-gras" night at Coney Island with them. Significantly, the first ride they go on is "Noah's Ark," a cheap commercialization of the biblical story Lorry has just been reading. Everything at Coney Island is of course a vulgar imitation of "the real thing." Dahlberg constantly emphasizes the qualities of artifice and illusion necessary for escape from the unhappy realities of life. "The moving-picture electric advertising signs flowed a sleazy nedick's chemise orange through the mist" (209). . . . "Some linoleum tiger lilies gleamed from the window of the florist next door" (210). . . . "The trains, the color of a loud pair of shoes, tap down the tracks and moving-picture their oleomargerine lights against the broken-down detective-story houses underneath them" (211). . . . "Outside the trumpet-flare of the mardi-gras lights, the two dames turned back" (212). One could easily continue to point out this imagery of artificiality throughout this chapter that culminates in Lorry's ride through a Coney Island version of "The Slums of Paris"—a ride in an imitation boat though an artificial canal:

> The Slums of Paris flickered again. The faked-up grotto made of wood and canvas recalled Calvary cemetery, all those boulders which formed a wall around the graveyard and which were so intensely natural as to suggest artifice. All the desolation and dizziness of artifice, of contrived unreality swirling in his brain and in the pit of his stomach like the round-and-round carousel. . . . He thought of his mother again, her head always a dissociated skull, her chin a slick poignant chip of soap, her body soap-sculpture; and whenever he thought of her now, Calvary rose up before him and crucified him until he wished she was dead. (236–37)

Here the themes of artificiality and death become one; for, in order to make his life livable, Lorry must construct artifice and unreality to avoid a bitter confrontation with things as they are and with death as the only certainty man can know. Ironically, he must escape life in order to live it; and death, of course, is the ultimate escape.

But, despite this realization, Lorry continues to seek meaning and purpose in life—this time in a search for his past. His return to the orphanage in Cleveland, however, ends in disillusionment and despair. The black crepe For Sale sign which greets him upon arrival at the orphanage entrance is symbolic of the emptiness of his past, and he finds the asylum run down and deserted—"it lay scattered and dumped like bones" (255). Only the memory can remain, and it is perhaps in the reconstruction of that memory that we can discover whatever meaning or purpose his life can have. But, after a brief reverie, the Wordsworthian emotion "recollected in tranquility" offers only momentary respite. Lorry concludes his visit to the orphanage with the realization that "He was in no place and no place was in him. He had nowhere to go" (271).

These lines seem to echo the sentiments expressed at the conclusion of *Bottom Dogs,* and we realize that Lorry's travel and his experiences have not altered the essential aimlessness of his life. The inevitable death of his mother in the final section of the novel leaves him totally isolated from his past; and *From Flushing to Calvary* closes, like its predecessor, on a note of drift and despair. His plans for the future are vague and uncertain; and the thought of hitting the road again, moving from one dreary city to another, leaves him indifferent. In the final scene, Lorry walks pointlessly through Washington Square Park singing an orphan-asylum hymn; and the last two lines of the hymn end the novel with bitter irony: *"'neath its folds, defeat unknown, triumph, triumph crowns our glorious way"* (293).

In a letter to Theodore Dreiser dated January 4, 1938, Dahlberg writes: "I have no quarrel with naturalism as such; but I want a purificatory naturalism. If our times is a gargantuan vomit I will loathe it but not grovel in it. I will face it but not immerse in it. I won't add another vomit bath to it."[7] The phrase "purificatory naturalism" perhaps best captures the spirit of Dahlberg's early phase. Clearly autobiographical in origin, the story of Lorry Lewis enabled Dahlberg to emerge from the dilemma we find Lorry in at the end of the narrative. The lack of hope and the almost total despair in *Bottom Dogs* and in *From Flushing to Cal-*

*vary* may arouse revulsion in some readers, but this cathartic revulsion creates in them a new awareness of the "lower depths" of human existence. Having written these books, Dahlberg could turn to "lower depths" of a different kind—the rising sceptre of Hitlerism and the apathy of America's middle classes.

CHAPTER 3

# Political Interlude

THE years 1933–36 were the most politically active of Dahlberg's life; for, like so many writers of the era, he saw hope in the promise of Marxism as a counter to the grim economic depravity of the mass of America's workers. More than this, however, his European experience gave him a firsthand look at the growing menace of fascism which he had quite early diagnosed as the major threat of the period to human values. His visit to Germany in 1933 at the time of the Reichstag fire convinced him that the state was already beginning to engulf the individual, and it precipitated a period of political activism that is unique in his career. Shortly after his return to the United States, he wrote an article for the New York *Times*[1] which accurately forecasted Hitler's reign of terror to a degree that must have later surprised even veteran political analysts.

Dahlberg intended to stir the American conscience about the events in Nazi Germany in a novel, *Those Who Perish.* In 1935 he was an organizer of the Marxist-oriented American Writer's Congress which attempted to assess the role of the writer as a political propagandist. Some years later, Dahlberg regretted his flirtation with the Marxist ethic, ruefully suggesting that Marxism "set back American literature for at least a century." [2] But at the time, it seemed to him, as it did to many American intellectuals of the 1930's, to be the wave of the future and the salvation of man's destiny. Thus, we find him concluding an introduction to Kenneth Fearing's *Poems* in thoroughly dogmatic Marxist terms: "His poetry, for those who are still wavering, is one more piece of documented evidence of the horrible mutilation of human dreams and nobleness under capitalism." [3]

But this rhetoric is rarely found anywhere else in Dahlberg's work. It is significant, I think, that he is *not* among the writers included in the influential anthology, *Proletarian Literature in the*

*United States,* published in 1935. Although he sympathized with the Marxist intention, he never could quite wholly devote himself to the cause because he sensed that it would swallow the man. The period seems more vigorously "anti-Fascist" than it is "pro-Marxist," and the tone of the only major literary work he wrote during these years reinforces this contention.

## I Those Who Perish

Whatever the esthetic shortcomings of Dahlberg's only propagandistic novel may be, *Those Who Perish* is an important social document because it is probably the first anti-Nazi novel to appear in this country.[4] Moreover, the novel is certainly the first major literary work to deal with the question of the ultimate responsibility others must share for permitting the Nazi atrocities to occur. The theme seems a commonplace one today after the Nuremberg and the Eichmann trials, the controversy over Rolf Hoccuth's *The Deputy,* and many other plays, movies, and novels which have dealt with this subject. But when we recall that Dahlberg's indictment was written in 1934 while the events were occurring, the book must strike us as prophetic.

The target of attack in the novel is not the Nazis themselves but the American Jews who remained complacent while their brothers and sisters were being persecuted as a prelude to the wholesale slaughter which followed. After Dahlberg's return from Germany in 1933, he became active on the executive board of the National Committee for the Defense of Political Prisoners. *Those Who Perish,* an outgrowth of this experience, seems intended as an impassioned plea to move the American Jewish community into action before the disastrous consequences of the Hitlerian purge. Under particular attack is what Dahlberg diagnosed as the tendency of the American Jews of the period to put economic concerns above human concerns at a time when economic self-interest clearly needed to be sacrificed in order to put pressure on Germany to relent in its persecution of the Jews. The central issue in the early part of the novel is the question of an economic boycott of German goods that is proposed by a group known as the United Jewish Committee.

A representative of the committee, Lawrence Scheer, is sent to the Community House, a suburban New York Jewish organization, to convince its members to support the boycott. Scheer, however, turns out to be something less than a passionate advocate of the proposal, and he tells the group that he is both "for and against" the boycott. He rationalizes Nazi actions in the name of anti-communism and suggests that the Nazis are indeed "the last dyke against Communism." "Our job," he tells the members of the Community House, "is to temporarily weaken but not to destroy that dyke." [5]

Joshua Boaz, the novel's central character and the director of the Community House, becomes enraged by Scheer's speech and by the reaction which it elicits. Most of the members find the for-and-against position a comfortable one because it permits them to condemn the moral atrocities of Nazism without having to make any personal economic sacrifice. As one of the members puts it, "I'm a manufacturer of broad-cloth for shirts. If we boycott German goods, I don't see how I can get the dyes I need. American dye-manufacturers are holding us up. We should restrict the boycott to a moral attack, an indignation program that will arouse public sentiment all over the world. I say, put the boycott on a spiritual plane and don't turn it into a sordid business" (37).

Ironically, a mood of rampant anti-Semitism permeates the meeting. These American middle-class Jews manifest the same hatred and bigotry that the group is supposed to be condemning. The president of the Community House, Harry Rosenzweig, secretly admits to himself that he "was not altogether sorry that they [the German Jews] were getting a lesson at the hands of the Nazis" (34). Another member evinces an incredible lack of human concern by remarking, "so there'll be 600,000 Jews less in the world, so what!" (35). Still another states, "I never liked the German Jews, a bunch of apostates" (35). These attitudes prove too much for Boaz to take: "Not since I was the director of the B'nai Brith Anti-Defamation League in Chicago have I heard such anti-semitic rantings, such libel and slander, and this time it is the Jews who are the worst Jew-baiters I have ever heard" (38). He bitterly condemns the proceedings and storms out of the meeting. The group then agrees to support the for-and-against position, and the chapter ends on the note of their total lack of human concern. Harry Rosenzweig leaves the meeting "certain . . . that he was For and Against. But the speaker had used such high-up

English, such refined language, that Rosenzweig could not remember just what the Representative from the United Jewish Committee had been for and against" (51).

The remainder of *Those Who Perish* centers around the actions of the three main characters—Boaz; Regina Gordon, his mistress and his daughter's tutor; and Eli Melamed, a "down and out" Jew who appeals to Boaz for financial assistance. Both Boaz and Regina are the parents of cretin daughters, and this mutual concern brings them together in a more meaningful relationship than either is able to achieve in his marriage. Each of the three main characters has a tragic sense of the present, and each longs for a less troublesome past before the grim realities of their present lives became so intractable. In order to survive in a world which cares little about human feelings, each is forced to compromise his or her integrity and cultural heritage.

In the company of anti-Semitic gentiles, Melamed joins in the growing chorus of anti-Jewish remarks in order to feel "one of the crowd," to escape being despised as an outsider. Both Boaz and Regina are forced to substitute politics for culture; and neither feels entirely comfortable with the rhetoric of communism. Of Regina, Dahlberg writes, "Had she lived in a less tragic age, her conversational vocabulary would have included more such names and words as Gautier, George Moore, Richard [*sic*] Burton, Anatole France, onyx, sapphire, Oscar Wilde, and less of Bolshevism, Marx, Lenin, and Fascism. As it was, the one vocabulary canceled the other, and the two rarely, if ever, co-existed in her consciousness" (71). For Dahlberg, as well as for Regina, the political imperatives of the 1930's made a broadly based cultural humanism difficult to sustain.

Toward the end of the novel, Joshua Boaz comments, "My moral reflexes were so slow . . ." (221); and in this comment lies the crux of the book's message. All three of the main characters die, unable to cope with the exigencies of a cruel, impersonal world. Melamed leaps from the Brooklyn Bridge in despair; Boaz has a heart attack when he mistakes Regina's daughter for his own recently deceased child; Regina then poisons both her daughter and herself. This macabre ending, which is indeed melodramatic, is an appropriate one; for, symbolically, Dahlberg seems to be saying that humanistic morality died in America when we remained silent about what was going on in Germany and permitted the Hitlerian menace to gain momentum. Boaz and Regina particularly are the "those who perish" of the book's title—humanists born in the wrong age. What Dahlberg tells us about Regina applies to Boaz as well: "Regina Gordon had lived her life and emotions in one age and was implacably trapped in another" (227). The universality of the "Fascist temperament" and their realization of this universality, proves too much for either Regina or Boaz to endure. "You think that Fascism was invented purely and simply to exterminate the Jews and that war, murder, and Nazism are barbarities unknown to the gentle Jewish soul" (231), she shouts in moral outrage at Boaz.

Together, they are symbolic of an earlier concerned generation that is out of step with the realities of the time and is doomed to pass from the earth without legacy: "so both of them had produced sterile, produceless, cretins. Neither he nor she could generate anything but barrenness and famine. It would have been much better to destroy them at the beginning than to encumber a world already fruitless and cretin enough. . . . Both she and Joshua had died when Deborah and Irma had been born" (236–37). "To live up to the hilt of one's times," Regina Gordon remarks before taking her daughter's life and her own, "is to have the saber of those times drawn against one" (241). Unable to face the inevitability of the Fascist ascension, the humanistic temper, or so it seemed to Dahlberg in 1934, was threatened with extinction.

Although Dahlberg wrote *Those Who Perish* as an "avowed Marxist," it is again not quite accurate to interpret this third book of the "proletarian" novels as an exercise in Marxist polemics. Anticapitalistic in its attack on the greed and exploitation of the American economic system and certainly anti-Fascist, the "proletarian" label simply does not suffice in the more positive sense of supplying literary propaganda for Marxism. Boaz, who is clearly the most sympathetic character in the novel and the one who comes closest to being a spokesman for Dahlberg himself, remarks that "my principal objection to Communism is that it's noisy, and as you put it, exhibitionistic" (80). Consistent with Dahlberg's later position in *Can These Bones Live* and *The Flea of Sodom,* he is critical of the Marxist denial of man's cultural potential and of its tendency to debase the best in man rather than to elevate the worst. Though he proposes no clear alternative in the novel, Dahlberg's sympathies seem to lie with a broader-based cultural humanism which would free man of the narrow confines of a rigid economic theory, either capitalistic or communistic.

Thus, even at this early stage in Dahlberg's career, we can sense the disillusionment with Marxism that becomes an important part of his later work. In an interview many years later, he remarked: "After I had finished the book [*Those Who Perish*] and considered the fusty prose which I employed, I was so disheartened that I realized that dialectical Marxism was very baleful to literature." [6] And it is true that few literary modes have dated as quickly as the propagandistic Marxist novels of the 1930's. Even in the best of the genre—Robert Cantwell's *The Land of Plenty* (the heavy irony of the title is typical) and Mary Heaton Vorse's *Strike!*—the oversimplified solutions to complex human problems strike us today as naïve and unconvincing.

The proletarian writers did, however, inject an intense social concern into the materials of American fiction, and with this aspect of their writing Dahlberg's novel seems most in concert. *Those Who Perish* is a significant book in the intensity of its outcry and in its depiction of the caverns of human despair which man was called upon to endure during the post-depression years. The kind of endurance Joshua Boaz faces is of a different nature than that of Lorry Lewis, but it is endurance nonetheless, and all three of Dahlberg's early works deal with what Alfred Kazin calls "the lower depths in America." [7] Boaz "stood aghast at what he felt he and all humanity had yet to endure, today and tomorrow and forever, until death: to be forever pushing oneself into something else, lashing oneself into new activities, details, plans, business meetings. To perform all those acts man must do, because it is even more hallucinatory to do nothing . . ." (88).[8] *Those Who Perish* remains an accurate literary record of the limits of man's moral endurance.

## II *American Writers' Congress*

Perhaps feeling that literary activity alone was not enough to protest the social inequities of the 1930's and to curb the dangerous spread of fascism, Dahlberg became active as an organizer and participant in the first American Writers' Congress held at the New School for Social Research in New York during April, 1935. The Congress was a response to a "call" which had been issued by a group of prominent writers with leftist sympathies and which had been sent to almost all notable writers in America. The organizers of the meeting proposed

> that a Congress of American revolutionary writers be held in New York City on April 26, 27 and 28, 1935; that to this Congress shall be invited all writers who have achieved some standing in their respective fields; who have clearly indicated their sympathy with the revolutionary cause; who do not need to be convinced of the decay of capitalism, of the inevitability of revolution. . . .
>
> This Congress will be devoted to exposition of all phases of a writer's participation in the struggle against war, the preservation of civil liberties and the destruction of fascist tendencies everywhere. It will develop the possibilities for wider distribution of revolutionary books and the improvement of the revolutionary press, as well as the relations between revolutionary writers and bourgeois publishers and editors. It will provide technical discussion of the literary applications of Marxist philosophy and of the relations between critic and creator. It will solidify our ranks.[9]

At the meeting, the group formed the Marxist-oriented League of American Writers, headed by Waldo Frank. Dahlberg was named to the National Council of the organization along with thirty-eight other writers including Nelson Algren, Van Wyck Brooks, James T. Farrell, Kenneth Fearing, Lewis Mumford, and Richard Wright.

A vigorous discussion of the role of the writer in relation to the revolutionary movement occurred at the meeting, and papers were read on various aspects of the subject. Dahlberg, responding to the phrase "the destruction of fascist tendencies everywhere" in the "call," read a paper entitled "Fascism and Writers" and was a spirited participant in the debate. An extremely revealing document, this paper is essentially contiguous with his later critical positions, despite his break with Marxist ideology. What he argues, and later proposes with a great deal more erudition and power in *Can These Bones Live,* is that literature become involved with moral questions, and that it not ignore human concerns. Overly preoccupied with esthetics, American writers, he felt, had been sidestepping the crucial moral problems of the day and were producing a literature that was out of touch with realities. "One can say," he remarked, "that while Clemenceau was writing to Woodrow Wilson during the World War, 'a drop of oil is worth a drop of blood,' and Sir Henry Deterding, the British oil magnate, was subsidizing the Wrangels and Kolchaks to gain possession of the Baku wells, a great many writers were intoning, 'A rose is a rose is a rose.' " [10]

Dahlberg then discusses the disillusionment which writers faced following World War I. American writers particularly, who went to war to "make the world safe for democracy," emerged from the experience bitter and disillusioned; and they produced a literature which is passionately opposed to war. He cites E. E. Cummings's *The Enormous Room* and John Dos Passos's *Three Soldiers,* among other novels, as those which reflect the growing bitterness and antiwar fervor that was a result of the military experience.

By 1929, according to Dahlberg, a social consciousness began developing in our literature. A group of noted novelists—Dreiser, Waldo Frank, and Josephine Herbst among them—traveled to the Soviet Union and emerged from this experience with a new faith in communism as man's only hope for the future. Dahlberg heralds this development, for at the time, communism and the humanistic temper seemed compatible to him. But more important than a dedication to communism, he urges writers to direct their energies to exposing and attacking fascism. He suggests, echoing a central theme of *Those Who Perish,* that the appeal of fascism is not restricted to any peculiarities of nationality or culture but thrives through deception of the masses by power-hungry men. The writer's role is particularly important, says Dahlberg, because "in order to hold the workers, farmers and middle classes whom they have deceived, they [Fascist governments] must gain the support of the writers." [11]

After a brief survey of Fascist-oriented literature, Dahlberg concludes his paper with a discussion of anti-Semitism. He suggests (again with *Those Who Perish* clearly in mind) that anti-Semitism is one of the most important problems contemporary writers must grapple with. In as Marxist a tone as his writing ever has had, he proposes that "A writer who cannot completely embrace the cause of the oppressed racial minorities, Negro and Jew and others, will never be able to fight for or enter the new socialist order for which every civilized human being must contend." [12]

Finally, he summons writers to devote their work to "the working class of America and the world." [13]

These concluding polemics have a "workers-of-the-world-unite" flavor that is out of key with the main thrust of Dahlberg's remarks here and in his later work. But the body of the paper, which deals with the threat of fascism, clearly relates to his concept of the dangers of the state as presented in his essays on Randolph Bourne and Thoreau in his later critical works. The subjugation of the individual to abstract entities he clearly perceived here as the central danger of fascism; he was not yet to perceive the same kind of threat in communism; but that was to come quickly in *Can These Bones Live* and *The Flea of Sodom.*

During the last few sessions of the congress, which consisted of an informal discussion of the various papers and related topics, Dahlberg urged that writers become more passionate about their writing and about social concerns. The revolutionary movement, he felt, could rescue the writer from the neglect he faced in bourgeois society. But he must have an impassioned belief in the efficacy of literature and make a determined effort to create a truly revolutionary literature. "You can't build up a literature without passion," he argued, "and if you have no passion, you had better stop writing." [14]

In its concluding meeting, the congress officially formed the League of American Writers and passed a series of resolutions protesting the suppression of civil rights, "the burning of schools and the closing of institutions of higher learning and the murder of intellectuals in Cuba, . . . against William Randolph Hearst and all his publications," and also demanding release of revolutionary intellectuals throughout the world.[15] The congress adjourned as James T. Farrell suggested that the writers conclude their work by singing the "International."

## III Bitch Goddess

In the spring 1936, issue of *Signature* magazine, the first chapter of Dahlberg's abortive fourth novel appeared. Why he never completed the work is difficult to know, although, given its apparent Marxist tone, his growing disillusionment with Marxism is perhaps reason enough. Then, too, he had already begun work on *Do These Bones Live,* a book which required an enormous amount of reading in American literature and in the Classics. It is easy to imagine that Dahlberg's engagement by this new work superseded his interest in the novel and forced him to set it aside. Whatever the reason, he completed only the first chapter of *Bitch Goddess* and permanently (at least to the present) set aside his novelistic inclinations. After this last attempt at a novel, his work moved in the direction of literary criticism, mythology, memoir, autobiography, poetry, and aphorism.

Though we have very little of the novel and though it is impossible to know in what direction Dahlberg intended to develop it, there are a few aspects of *Bitch Goddess* which deserve our attention because of the light they shed on the main line of Dahlberg's literary development. The first chapter describes the life of Eugene Wertheim, a struggling, young, free-lance writer, and his roommate, Alex Salter, a struggling, young, free-lance painter. Together they live in a decrepit fifth-floor, cold-water flat in Greenwich Village. Perpetually threatened with eviction by their greedy and boorish capitalistic landlord, a man named Lumsky, they survive, half starving, by the little Salter manages to earn selling his paintings. Little occurs in the chapter. There is a brief flashback relating Wertheim's experiences in Paris when he was "taken for a ride" by a group of French anarchists seeking to punish an American for the death of Sacco and Vanzetti; and, toward the end of the chapter, Salter and Wertheim are visited by two bohemian artists who engage them in a discussion of whether or not art should be placed in the service of the masses.

Taken by itself, there is little in this brief excerpt which engages our interest. But, when we relate it to Dahlberg's other novels, it gains significance because it seems a continuation of the life of Lorry Lewis, this time called Eugene Wertheim; and, had Dahlberg completed the novel, we may well have had a *Bottom Dogs* trilogy. Lorry's literary leanings had been suggested in *From Flushing to Calvary*. Eugene is Lorry grown-up; and, determined to become a successful writer, he is thwarted by the commercialism required to achieve success. The references to Eugene's mother are strikingly reminiscent of the Lorry-Lizzie relationship in the early works. Here she has not yet died (as Dahlberg's actual mother had not yet died, though he wrote of Lizzie's death in *From Flushing to Calvary*), but the thought of her impending death weighs heavily on Eugene's mind: "he thought of his poor mouldering mother. And as he saw her in her coffin, the mute unrecorded dust of her hair, his throat locked. . . . He had wept because some day his own mother would be no more and then he would not exist."[16] The fear of permanent separation, so prominent in the later pages of *From Flushing to Calvary,* is again apparent here.

Another notable aspect of *Bitch Goddess* is the style. And what makes it notable is that it is so thoroughly unlike Dahlberg; for it is neither the Naturalistic journalism of the early novels nor the allusive resonant prose of the later works. The most striking thing about it is its Joycean cadence and technique, and stylistically this chapter seems the most derivative of Dahlberg's works. There are clipped, staccato sentences suggesting immediacy and quick movement: "Loud banging on the door. He rolled and unfolded in the blankets of his flesh. 'Open up or I'll call the police!' . . . The door slammed to. Upstairs. . . . It was morning. Churning against the perforated shade and the window frame. No. Later, earlier. Morning gray as a horse's hoof."[17]

Even more Joycean is the use of various rhetorical devices to achieve cadence and poetic effect. Dahlberg uses internal rhyme, alliteration, repetition, and a mock-heroic treatment of commonplace subject matter—all hallmarks of the Joycean mode. One brief passage makes use of all of these techniques and should serve to suggest Dahlberg's indebtedness to Joyce in this unfinished work:

> Where were his pants, where were the slops and slobs of pants of him, the bulbous rats of shoes, the socks, stale slivery spuds of socks, the watch and chain, somewhere in Davenport in hocks! no bad! not bad! but eat it! But to put the right and then the left leg through the tunnel of the trousers without coming into a head-on with the crotch, oh the delicate crotch, to make a botch of the delicate subtle crotch and then to give the fly to the index buttons. But choke the tap or else to the can I go. And if the foot slipped by the crotch there were the buttons so cold to the touch and must ridden with a thousand; then the shoes, what is more calamitous than breaking the shoelace, where greater defects, where a lousier piece of distintegration.[18]

It goes on like this, almost a parody of Joyce, yet one senses no satirical intent. It is the kind of prose Dahlberg was later to castigate so severely in *Truth Is More Sacred,* and it is indeed fortunate that his work took another direction after this brief flirtation with literary fashion.

Dahlberg was not long to remain "fashionable." The 1930's, though not the years of his major literary achievement, were important years for his development. His travels in Europe, his outrage at human injustice, and his determination to enlist art in the service of man place him squarely in the literary temper of the day. The experience of writing his three early works and his unfinished novel contributed to his narrative talent which blossoms anew in *Because I Was Flesh.* With our increasing interest in the decade of the 1930's, Dahlberg's early works deserve another look because they capture to a degree that few novels of the period do the literary and social climate of the depression years—the conflicts and interrelationships between art and society which so dominated the atmosphere of that very troubled decade.

CHAPTER 4

# Literary Skeletons

IN terms of quantity, the decade of the 1940's was one of modest literary activity for Dahlberg. He produced only two full-length works during these years, but they introduce us to a new stylistic sensibility. The first of these books, *Do These Bones Live* is a major achievement; and it ranks second only to *Because I Was Flesh* as Dahlberg's *magnum opus.* It has been called by Allen Tate an American "classic" [1] and is so, despite its limited readership. The other, *The Flea of Sodom,* is the most experimental work in the Dahlberg canon. Known by even fewer readers, it is nevertheless a good example of a fusion between the old Dahlberg and the new. Less successful than the work either before or after it, it is a puzzling book both thematically and stylistically. Together, however, these works introduce us to an Edward Dahlberg who has moved far beyond the Naturalistic limitations of the fiction of the 1930's, and who has become something of a phenomenon in our age of mass media—a man of letters.

## I Can These Bones Live

Dahlberg's major work of literary criticism was published in 1941 under the title *Do These Bones Live.* Reissued and somewhat revised, it appeared in England in 1947 with a preface by Sir Herbert Read which, as Harold Billings notes, marks "the daybreak of critical appreciation of the work of Dahlberg's maturity." [2] The English edition was entitled *Sing O Barren,* taken from the title of one of the essays in the work. A third revision, published in America in 1960, was entitled *Can These Bones Live.* The title of The American Edition is taken from Ezekiel 37:3, and in every major Bible the interrogative is translated as "can." It is surely possible, however, that the original title was either a mistranslation or a misquotation; and, if the latter, the change in the later edition is quite understandable.

The context of the passage from Ezekiel suggests its application to American letters:

> The hand of the Lord was upon me, and carried me out in the spirit of the Lord, and set me down in the midst of the valley which was full of bones,
> And caused me to pass by them round about: and, behold, there were very many in the open valley; and, lo, they were very dry.
> And he said unto me, Son of man, can these bones live? And I answered, O Lord God, thou knowest.
> Again he said unto me, Prophesy upon these bones, and say unto them, O ye dry bones, hear the word of the Lord.

The full quotation reveals quite accurately the tenor of *Can These Bones Live:* it is a work of prophecy which takes American literature as its departure. More prosaically, it is a collection of critical essays, primarily on American literature, but not without reference to Shakespeare, Cervantes, Dostoevsky, and many other major figures of world literature.

A primary theme of the work is the lack of human concern which Dahlberg finds a lamentable tendency in America's letters from the Puritans through the proletarian Naturalists. Secondary themes are the fallacy of man's devotion to the state, the relationship of art to reality, the paucity of believable female characters in our literature, and the need for literature to draw upon myth and legend for images and symbols. If any doubts remain regarding Dahlberg's Marxist inclinations, clearly they are resolved in this work which is not only anti-Marxist throughout but critical of the influence of any kind of dogmatics upon literature.

Stylistically, the book demonstrates a clear turning away from the unadorned Naturalistic prose of the first three novels. For the first time we read the richly allusive style that has become the hallmark of Dahlberg's later writing. The stylistic shift is evident from the very first paragraph, and the reader of the earlier novels becomes immediately cognizant that Dahlberg has left his journalistic naturalism behind him. About as far from the "gutter vernacular" of *Bottom Dogs* as one can get are the introductory sentences of *Can These Bones Live* with their reverberating resonances from the world's literature:

> Truth, Good and Evil revolve like the perpetual wheel to which Ixion was bound. Tamburlaine, the "Scythian thief," sprinkles Asiatic lands with the brains of men, and thirsts for the far infinities of the Milky Way; unambitious and loving Hamlet, who can "be bounded in a nutshell, and count myself a king of infinite space," embitters the earth; Macbeth speaks truths from Gothic caves of terror; the evil and saturnine Ahab, soaked in a metaphysical revenge and in blood "older than the Pharaohs'," knows moral ecstasies as tender as ". . . let me look into a human eye; it is better than to gaze into the sea and sky; better than to gaze upon God." Resolve these ambiguities who can? [3]

Allen Tate has remarked "that one may learn more about the human condition of our time from this book than from a dozen labored sociological tracts." [4] Indeed, this quality of the various essays—what they reveal to us about the human condition—causes them to rise above the narrow confines of a strictly literary criticism. Dahlberg is far less concerned with the esthetic qualities of the works he discusses than he is with their continuing relevance. Only if our literary past helps us to grapple with the paradox and uncertainty of human experience can the "bones" of American literature live.

The book is divided into eight sections entitled, respectively, "The Man-eating Fable," "Thoreau and Walden," "Randolph Bourne: In the Saddle of Rosinante," "Can These Bones Live," "The Bridegroom's Ache," "The Cross and the Windmills," "Women," and "Superstition and Images." Sections four, five, seven, and eight are subdivided into smaller units which deal with some aspect of the larger topic. As these titles may suggest, the work has no overriding unity, but it touches on a number of interrelated themes in a somewhat arbitrary order.

"The Man-eating Fable," a short essay, deals with the ambiguity that is man's lot, particularly as reflected in *Hamlet, Macbeth,* and *Timon of Athens.* Man lives in an ambiguous world and cannot resolve the contradictions he finds all around him. "Truth, Good and Evil," as Dahlberg notes in the paragraph already quoted, "revolve like the perpetual wheel to which Ixion was bound"; and, in a Blakean phrase, Dahlberg concludes that "Good and evil are inseparable; beast and man are sewn together with the threads of heaven" (9). Yet man at his best, at his most creative, retains his idealism by remaining true to the dictates of his heart. The function of art, as Dahlberg sees it, is to record man's continuing attempt to transcend his limits and to *create* the meaning he so desperately needs if he is to maintain his rationality. These are the lessons that we derive from *Hamlet,* from *Macbeth,* and from *Timon,* despite the fact that each of these plays is a "man-eating fable" in which the quest for meaning devours the seekers: "But no matter how disenchanted man becomes, he does not forswear the legendary course of the heart. He cannot. Man pursues a desperado philosophy of gallant idealism, and lives and hopes and cankers with a defiant flourish. With inextinguishable fervor he ceaselessly creates his cycles of sonnets, music, art, ethics, and then with a chivalric irony wraps the WORMS in the GOLDEN FLEECE OF COLCHIS. This is his eternal battle of valiant desperation against all palpable and unknown limits" (7).

This theme, particularly the phrase "legendary course of the heart," strikes us as Lawrentian, and it would be easy to cite parallels between Dahlberg's position here and Lawrence's in *Studies in Classic American Literature.* But it would be equally easy to make too much of this relationship. There is a mystical quality in much of *Can These Bones Live,* but it is nowhere so primitivistic as Lawrence's "blood knowledge." Dahlberg's mysticism is informed and tempered by Classicism—by a deep commitment to the cultural heritage of the past. We must look to the heart, he argues, but we must look as well to art and literature because they enable us to know better what is in the heart.

The essay "Thoreau and *Walden*" is a re-evaluation of *Walden* in terms of its application to contemporary life. Like most of Dahlberg's criticism, it focuses on the moral aspect of the work—what Walden teaches us, how it is relevant, what application it has to our daily lives. As I have suggested earlier, the moralistic tenor of Dahlberg's critical remarks seems curiously out of touch with the main critical principles of our time; but his essay on Thoreau may give us cause to examine the foundations of our critical approach and to question whether or not discussions of form, structure, texture, imagery, and so on deserve more attention than the ideas, feelings, and meanings which literature conveys.

We have made Thoreau a saint of American letters, Dahlberg tells us; but we do not *experience* his work—we learn nothing from his thought. The central question Thoreau poses in his writing is one of the most important questions man must come to terms with in his daily experience: how to resist evil? "*Walden* . . . is the secular bible of our ethics. What it hints of—*how* to resist evil, society, patriotism, poverty and war—we dare no more neglect. How to resist? Therein lie all the morals and all the terror of this world" (13). After reading Dahlberg's essay, the reader must conclude it is ironic that we have honored Thoreau with kudos of literary acclaim (and in 1968 even a commemorative postage stamp) and have so consistently ignored the *meaning* of his work. This view is, of course, consistent with our reverence of many literary figures at the expense of their thought: "Sequester the writer, make him an 'early American' of a Golden Age of Letters, and you refuse him" (15). This fate, Dahlberg feels, Thoreau has suffered in our day; and, if we are to respond meaningfully to *Walden,* we must revivify the man and the ideas behind the work. "Thoreau is the parable which will never be experienced until America has transmuted the logic of *Walden* into the lore of the heart" (20).

*What* Thoreau teaches us is, in essence, the message of much Oriental thought: "The Brahmans never proposed courageously to assault evil, but patiently to starve it out" (24). Dahlberg sees Confucius, Thoreau, and Tolstoi as prophets of the doctrine of passive resistance which, he argues, is a far truer and more effective means of combating evil than opposing it with force and additional evils. We must put faith in man's mind and heart in the hope that they will direct his will and shape his future destiny. "Since it is the mind that is the vessel of all good and evil in the world, why is it that we so distrust its strength in opposing the violence at large today" (21), Dahlberg asks; and we still stutter to reply. *Walden,* he concludes, is a visionary book which can teach us to know and understand ourselves (for Dahlberg the *function* of all great literature) if we study it in terms of its meaning for our own lives, rather than as the prime example of the "renaissance" in American letters which occurred in the mid-nineteenth century.

The essay about Randolph Bourne which follows is a natural complement to one about Thoreau. Like Thoreau, Bourne saw the state as the precipitator of much of the world's evil. Dahlberg, writing at a time when Adolph Hitler was so vividly illustrating his point, vigorously agrees, and his chapter on Bourne is a diatribe against the antihumanistic tendencies of the state which devour the individual and create wars and strife for economic gain and political power. "Not since Thoreau has any American save Randolph Bourne shown such lucid anger against the mummery of the State" (34). Yet Bourne, one of our few "truthful" writers in Dahlberg's eyes, is largely unknown as a part of our literary heritage because he gave his allegiance to no specific dogma or credo.

And here Dahlberg, with his eye surely on his own flirtation with Marxism, sees devotion to abstract doctrine as a dangerous and harmful inclination, for "All dogmas lead men to the Abyss; doctrine is the enemy of vision and the denial of the past" (35). Man, as Thoreau and Bourne taught, must act and react by the dictates of his own conscience and heart. Though Bourne's literary reputation has risen a good deal since 1941, this essay makes us feel that we have not yet fully assessed his importance. "One of the first things a devoted reader of *Do These Bones Live* will do," writes Jonathan Williams, "is procure a copy of *The History of a Literary Radical and Other Papers. . . .*"[5]

The title essay, "Can These Bones Live," is a survey of American literature which laments the solitude and alienation of the American writer, his lack of human contact, his devotion to realism at the expense of idealism, and his tendency to deny the past by making a fetish of originality. The longest essay in the collection, it is divided into eight subsections, each dealing with a major figure or theme in American literature.

The first of these, "Ishmael," is a discussion of the isolation of our nineteenth-century writers. Dahlberg argues that the aloneness of our major writers has had an enormous impact on our literature. "But so apart and incommunicable have been our own poets," he writes, "that we search for letters, for buried mementos and fragments of conversations to disclose whether Herman Melville had even heard of *Leaves of Grass,* whether Poe and Melville had met or whether *Moby Dick* was known to the Brahmans. Could there be a more melancholy concealment than the verse of Emily Dickinson, hid in the domesticated sarcophagus of a drawer—'snug in seraphic cupboards' " (43).

The separation of Americans from one another, he suggests, began with the Puritans who lived separate, sheltered lives, confiding only in their diaries and journals. There are few warm, human friendships of record during our Colonial period. Melville, Poe, and Hawthorne are the heirs of this tradition of apartness. Dahlberg depicts them as literary hermits whose writings suffer from their authors' paucity of human relationships. In addition, the isolation of our writers has contributed to their denial of the past. Such a charge seems difficult to sustain, particularly in the case of Hawthorne; but Dahlberg shifts ground a bit and cites primarily Poe and Whitman. Working separately with little communication between one another, our writers became obsessed by the desire to be original. Since human wisdom is cumulative, originality works against the creation of a meaningful literature. Some of our nineteenth-century authors, however—Emerson, Melville, the Boston Brahmans—"had the canny wisdom to steal their truths. . . . Imagine the aphorisms of Emerson without Plato, Shakespeare, Marcus Aurelius, Plutarch or Hegel" (50).

This essay contains some of the most remarkable prose Dahlberg has written, embodying all of the best qualities of the resonant style that characterizes his later work. Witness the following moving lament, an epitaph for Herman Melville:

> Ugly, bald dirt, as though cast down his ghostly gullet, lies upon Herman Melville. He is in Woodlawn Cemetery, that PIT OF ACHERON betwixt the subway terminus and the hither fringes of Yonkers, cankered with graying curls of dust from the yards of monument makers and palled with bitter macadam and the orchidaceous fumes of automobile gasoline. Is it not fitting, so American, that the most astonishing genius that ever came out of the Western Hemisphere should be so uncleanly slabbed in mean, cheap dirt, not among the pitiable poor, but with the common drab bulk of rightly unremembered dead. Look upon his sparse tombstone and read the frugal inscription written thereon, "OCCUPATION WRITER"; then utter aloud the pity for the artist, that Hamlet so dolorously sighs forth before his father's apparition, "Alas! Poor Ghost." (45)

Under the heading, "Sanctified Lies," Dahlberg next lashes out at the sterility of literary criticism in America. He begins by noting that "We have not lacked poets but what we have most mournfully missed are critics" (51). The harshest invective is leveled at what Dahlberg calls the "sterile grammarians" of American letters, our academic critics who, under the guise of a camouflaged literary chauvinism or "scientific" critical analysis, have distorted our notion of the true worth and meaning of our literature. Meaningful criticism must be an act of "creative faith." It becomes self-destructive when it substitutes academic platitudes and pseudo-scientific jargon for a deeply felt response to literature in terms of what it can reveal to us about the nature of man. Our critics have not acknowledged this important aspect of literature, and "the critical humbug continues, disguised as scientific or aesthetic or proletarian analyses of literature. There is no more boring or feckless hoax than the aesthetic-scientific vocabulary" (52).

Dahlberg concludes this section with a statement of his own critical position, a statement which Herbert Read cites in the preface as the essence of Dahlberg's faith: "There are no abstract truths—no Mass Man, no proletariat. There is only Man. When the Pulse has been nailed upon the crossbeams, lo, Reason gives up its viable breath and becomes a wandering ghostly Error. Truth and folly are ever about to expire, so that we, like our beloved Sancho Panza, kneeling at the deathbed of Don Quixote, must always be ready to go out to receive the holy communion of cudgels and distaffs for the rebirth of the Pulse" (55). Devotion to the individual and to reason informed by and infused with feeling —and not to collectivism, dogma, or a heartless rationality— emerge as the central tenets of Dahlberg's humanism.

In "The Flesh Refused," Dahlberg examines further the continuing impact of Puritanism on American writing. He began this essay by suggesting that the apartness of America's authors can be traced to their Puritan roots. Here he holds the Puritans responsible for denying, or at least ignoring, man's sexuality. Our Colonial writers repressed sexuality in their work by writing about nature: "The Puritan's churchly slaying of the sexual organs . . . was a furtive and diabolical worship of seedtime, spring and copulation" (56). The literature which emerged from this heritage, Dahlberg feels, has been essentially a denial of man through a "renunciation of the carnal heart" (56).

There is a paradox in this evaluation of our literary tradition. For, while Dahlberg is critical of the fact that "In almost a hundred years of American literature we do not have one feeding, breeding, sexual male" and "no ripe women" (59), he next levels his attack at our Naturalistic writers for emphasizing man's bestial nature at the expense of his spirit. After indicting American literature for denying the flesh, he now attacks Naturalism for groveling in it. The Naturalist's credo he regards as primarily a reaction to our Puritan heritage—perhaps more accurately, an overreaction. "But all holiness ends, as in *The Brothers Karamazov,* in the unspeakable stench of the corpse of Father Zossima" (66). The Naturalists, according to Dahlberg, have created the "Zossima's corpse" of American literature, and man emerges from the Naturalistic novel stripped of his nobility and dignity as "nothing but matter in motion loathing itself" (67).

The paradox is somewhat resolved in the section entitled "The Helmet of Mambrino." Like the famous barber's basin which appeared to Don Quixote a decorative and noble military helmet, art must partake of the "real" and the "ideal" at the same time. Realism is restrictive because it simply copies the world without ennobling it. A literature which simply mirrors an age is fulfilling only a part—Dahlberg would suggest the minor part—of its purpose. Shakespeare's plays may tell us a good deal about Elizabethan England, but they are important to us for what they tell us about human nature—its potential and its shortcomings. The ideal and the real are the polar tensions which operate in all art, and our greatest artists are able to reconcile the two: "Rembrandt's HAND is a concrete, fleshly human limb, and also an IDEAL, just as the barber's basin is to Sancho Panza what it optically represents as well as the HELMET OF MAMBRINO" (72). American literature must neither grovel in the flesh nor deny it; but like the plays of Shakespeare and the novels of Cervantes, it should present us with both the real and the ideal. To the degree which it has failed to depict the tensions between these two aspects of the human experience, it has fallen short of the world's great literature.

Another limitation of our "proletarian" literature, particularly is its lack of imagery or literary referents. If we strip man of image, metaphor, myth, ritual, and allusion, Dahlberg asserts, we deny his meaning: "Sociologic, proletarian literature is almost imageless; there are no stars, nights or dawns, no nature to touch, soften or ennoble man" (74). This position accurately describes the shift in Dahlberg's own style, so evident in *Can These Bones Live.* Though his earlier novels, as we have seen, are not quite so devoid of imagery and metaphor as the proletarian novels he describes, certainly the allusive prose in *Can These Bones Live* illustrates a literary temper that Dahlberg finds so lacking in the class-conflict novels of the 1930's. The "proletarian eucharist" (as he entitles this section) depicted in these novels is devoid of wine and gives us only the bread. And man, of course, cannot live by bread alone.

The final two sections of the long essay, "Can These Bones Live," deal with Hemingway and Faulkner and with the limitations of regionalism in literature. The major weakness Dahlberg finds in the novels of Hemingway and Faulkner is that the life processes are reversed in their work: these novels are negations of life rather than affirmations of it. Despite the fact that our academic critics have exalted them to the front rank of modern writers, both are basically Naturalists whose writing suffers from the limitations of the Naturalistic vision. Like Frank Norris, Jack London, and the proletarian novelists, they have overreacted to our Puritan heritage: "In the Puritan Christian cosmogony spirit was not rooted in flesh, just as now matter performs and behaves as though mind were not of it. The demented dervish of MATTER goes on without a past, a tradition or a memory" (78). Unable to relate our literature to a tradition, our writers have become cultists of place; therefore, many of our literary masterpieces are rooted in place, bounded by geographical limits. This characteristic has restricted American writers because it has worked against a concern for what is universal in the human experience. Dahlberg warns that "The artist who cravenly submits to time, place and space confesses his own limits" (80). Though we have had "artists of memory" in America—Poe, Melville, and Emily Dickinson—our major tradition has been the exultation of place; and American literature has suffered because of it.

The impact of the person of Jesus upon our literature is assessed in Section V, "The Bridegroom's Ache." Too often writers have substituted doctrine and dogma for the true meaning of Christ's life, which Dahlberg suggests has nothing to do with either. What emerges, however, from Dahlberg's interpretation of the essence of Christ's life is a paradox—both a denial of the flesh and a celebration of it. While Christ denounced the flesh, he made his own body and blood the focal point of Christian worship. This paradox has permeated all of the literature which grows out of the Christian tradition: "Dogma and denial, Calvary or Nature, trampled the throat of poets and visionaries; doctrine doomed the flower, fruit and savor of their blood" (95). Jesus was an enigma; Christian doctrine is paradoxical. In an attempt to resolve these difficulties, writers have emphasized the trappings which surround the man instead of attempting to comprehend the contradictory lessons of his life: "Jesus the bridegroom has perished; but the dogma, the ambiguous statutes, have endured: the nails, the cross, the hyssop, the dirty paraphernalia of sorrow, horror and belief have remained" (91).

Dahlberg's essay on *Don Quixote*, "The Cross and the Windmills," reveals to us the inner core of Cervantes's novel in fewer words than any explication of which I know. It is an excellent complement to the essay on Christ, because Dahlberg's reading of Cervantes, as suggested by the title of the essay, demonstrates many parallels between Don Quixote and Christ. Both the story of Christ and the tale of the Knight of the Sorrowful Countenance are parables of man's quest for ideals in a world which works against the pursuit of them. Both Christ and Don Quixote thought it essential for man to live a noble life—to attempt to fulfill his hopes and aspirations. The paradox both must contend with is that man lives in an ignoble world. The irony of the human condition is summed up perfectly in the life of the Man of La Mancha who "must affirm what is not, Dulcinea, giants, armies, the Helmet of Mambrino, since the common mass will forever deny what IS: Don Quixote, Sancho Panza and Christ" (113). Dahlberg depicts Christ and Don Quixote as dreamers who sought to raise life above the crass and the vulgar. They are the epitome of human aspiration which gives life whatever meaning it has. The conflict between these aspirations and the limitations of the real world is the stuff from which all great art is made.

American literature once again becomes the focal point of Dahlberg's discussion in the section simply entitled "Woman." Since this essay, Leslie Fiedler has given us in *Love and Death in the American Novel* [6] the idea that our literature has been somewhat lacking in the creation of believable female characters, and this view has become a critical commonplace. Dahlberg's analysis antedates Fiedler's by nineteen years, but they arrive at similar conclusions. In this essay Dahlberg laments the almost completely ephemeral character of the women depicted in our major literary works and their total absence in our greatest classics. *Moby Dick*, he reminds us, "is a human, cosmological Atlantic Tragedy, without one female figure," and he questions is there "not something drearily amiss?" (127). We may counter by suggesting that Melville's subject matter is hardly suited to the presentation of female characters—the presence of a woman aboard the *Pequod* would create all sorts of problems—but the indictment goes further than *Moby Dick*. Poe, he tells us, writes of ephemeral female phantoms; *Walden* is altogether devoid of women; "in Emily Dickinson, the appetites, sensual throbs, were always attributes of dew, the bee, a wagon" (127). Again, the Puritan heritage is called to task: "The books of the Puritan visionaries are the Lamb's testament; they lack the joyful knowledge that is the comedy of guile, habit, pleasure, the grape and wit of the house, the table and the bed" (127). The paucity of women in our letters is a rejection of our humanity, and a perversion of human motives and needs, for "Without woman, the Tree of Good and Evil cannot be tasted" (128). *Moby Dick,* which perfectly illustrates this rejection and perversion, shows us clearly how "Man, apart from woman, makes a carnage of his destiny; torn, he chases a dumb leviathan till death . . ." (128).

The title ("Sing O Barren") of the subsection of this essay devoted to Walt Whitman immediately indicates Dahlberg's critique of the most consistent "yea sayer" in our literature. His remarks about Whitman seem somewhat out of place in an essay about woman, although Dahlberg does see a rejection of the female in Whitman's poetry and comments on his homosexuality. More than this, however, his criticism of Whitman centers around the good gray poet's denial of evil and the darker aspects of human nature. By ignoring the "power of blackness," Whitman celebrates a lie and sings of barrenness. Whitman's mass "I" Dahlberg calls "the cold, algebraic multitude" (145); and he suggests that a literature which is not concerned with human suffering is empty and void of the great truths which all writers must come to terms with.

The essay on woman is concluded with a section entitled "False, Cressid! False, False, False!" which prescribes a return to the Classics if we are to discover a truthful depiction of the female in literature. He presents a catalogue of Classical heroines intended to remind us that literature must combine the ideal and the real as he had earlier suggested in "The Helmet of Mambrino." "Homer's ideal women," he writes, "are deep-bosomed; he says that Penelope's hand was 'plump,' but not 'thick' or 'crass' " (152). American writers should attempt to follow Homer's example. What we need are not more phantoms of sensuality, such as the heroines of even our most revered American "classics," but women who strike us as "true" in the same way that the female characters in the Classics do.

The final essay in *Can These Bones Live* takes up a theme introduced in the essays on Thoreau and Bourne. Entitled "Superstition and Images," it is a searing attack on the state which Dahlberg here calls "the penultimate superstition of mankind" (167). The only institution which rivals it in the art of mass deception, according to Dahlberg, is the church. Together these leviathans have forced man to deny his inner needs. They have substituted the idolatry of abstract credos and dogmas for warm human affection. If we are to discover meaning and point in life, we must turn inward and toward one another, rather than to the dictates of doctrine, either civil or religious. The concise sentence which concludes the volume summarizes this major theme as it occurs again and again in Dahlberg's work: "O, let man laugh the *gods* out of this world so that the heart can live in it!" (179).

It is more difficult to assess the totality of *Can These Bones Live* than it is to evaluate each of its parts. There is much repetition and some inconsistency; but, taken as a whole, the work is a major critical achievement. The contradictions we may find here shrink to mere quibbles in light of the total scheme. For what is consistent is a deeply felt humanism which laments the separation of men from one another and which demonstrates how this separation has penetrated our literature and made it less than it should be. Dahlberg's position throughout is essentially Aristotelian. He argues for a *media via* between the ideal and the real, between the flesh and the spirit, between a denial of evil and an affirmation of it, between submission to abstractions and egocentricity. It is not surprising that Thoreau emerges from these pages as the writer who most accurately represents Dahlberg's conception of what a writer should be, and what qualities his work should have. For more than most of our writers, Thoreau was able to achieve that balance in his work between these various extremes that Dahlberg sees as essential to major literary artistry.

What is surprising, however, is that Dahlberg makes no mention of the omission of the sexual experience in Thoreau's books, and their total lack of women. He cannot forgive Melville for leaving women out of *Moby Dick*, but is not at all critical of the same failing in *Walden*. Perhaps because the ideal and the real come together in *Walden* to a greater degree than any other work in American literature, Dahlberg overlooks many failings. Can these bones live? If we can have more writers like Thoreau, Dahlberg's answer is "Indeed they can."

## II *The Enigmatic* Flea

Dahlberg could not help being disappointed by the very little attention which his major critical work received. The first edition of *Do These Bones Live* sold only some 375 copies,[7] a disappointing figure even for someone of modest expectations. Undaunted, however, by this very meager reception to a work of seven years of labor and of an enormous amount of reading, he continued what he is fond of calling his "literary apprenticeship," studying the classics and steeping himself in the lore of ancient literatures. He continued a search for a new mode of writing, begun in *Do These Bones Live;* and in 1950, with little fanfare or notice, the "sedulously ignored little volume," [8] *The Flea of Sodom,* appeared.

An almost totally unclassifiable work, *The Flea of Sodom* begins as a parody of the proletarian novel, becomes a long essay infused with mythological allusions about the decadence of modern civilization, and concludes with a trio of parables lamenting the supremacy of the intellect at the expense of the spirit. Easily the most enigmatic of Dahlberg's books, it is also the most difficult. Jonathan Williams calls it paradoxically his "most unsatisfactory, provocative work," [9] and it is easy to agree with this judgment. The book *is* unsatisfactory in that its points are made opaquely, and its form is uncertain and lacks unity or continuity. On the other hand, it is provocative in the sense that it seems on the verge of generic invention; and its prose is as vigorous and challenging as anything Dahlberg has written. But the extensive allusion seems less natural and more affected than in *Can These Bones Live;* more often than not, the citations may strike the reader as somewhat arbitrary.

Part I of *The Flea of Sodom* is the beginning of a proletarian novel without the usual clichés and street vernacular that Dahlberg was so critical of in *Do These Bones Live.* He attempts to revitalize the genre by presenting the narrative in the new allusive style of his critical work. What emerges is not a novel at all but a parody of a novel, arrived at through a humorous juxtaposition of two styles and temperaments—the early Dahlberg and the late. This mixture often provides such incongruous effects as "The tables were occupied by a few marxists eating vile bread upon which they pasted mustard or ketchup. The spear of Menelaus never destroyed as many men as these happy sauces" (24).

Dahlberg's point in this section is the same one made with greater clarity and effectiveness in the earlier critical work: literature needs fable, ritual, myth, legend in order to thrive and be affecting. Since the proletarian novelists brought little or no fabulistic background to their writing, the literature they produced is sterile and uninspiring. Even more than this, it is, because of its emphasis on violence and human degradation, positively harmful. "The stalin authors and artists painted toilets, factories and proletarian women, without nuptual founts, instead of the face of Moses or Cybele. Men without a paternal land or gods, bring Mars to the people" (25).

The characters in the first section—and it is only this part of *The Flea of Sodom* which novelistically introduces characters—have such unlikely names as Ephriam Bedlam, Ajax Proletcult, Thersites Golem, and Andromache Lucy. William Carlos Williams has suggested that these names give the book an "archeologic flavor,"[10] and they certainly seem an attempt to elevate the proletarian novel beyond the drab, dull, and commonplace. But, in a novelistic context, the constant repetition of these labels diverts from the flow of the narrative and continually calls attention to itself. The juxtaposition of myth and proletarian subject matter, as illustrated by the character's names, is humorous; but the extension of this technique through some sixty pages sorely taxes the reader's sensibilities. There are many clever anecdotes related through this technique, such as the following passage describing a proletarian fund-raising affair:

> Pilate Agenda announced a cuckold buffet-supper. Andromache and Golem, who had been photographing Georgia crackers, came back with a Negro sharecropper whom they exhibited to Scranton and Pittsburgh steel workers. A Barcelona workmen's basement was rented to honor the Chinese people and to get money for the relief of the Koreans in the flood areas. Tickets were issued, with Agenda Russian caviar advertised on the back of each stub. Those that could not afford to purchase tickets counterfeited them on a private printing press. (42–43)

We may chuckle at the incongruity of the humor; but, as a method of writing, this technique shortly wears thin.

As if cognizant of the failure of the novelistic mode of *The Flea of Sodom,* Dahlberg abandons the narrative line altogether in the second section entitled "The Rational Tree"; and we move from the realm of the novel to the province of the essay with no apparent transition. The connection between the two sections is that both are critical of the "modern" temper, for Dahlberg explicitly laments the "progress" of man from an age of fable and myth to one of scientific fact and concludes that he is retrogressing rather than progressing. The blind pursuit of knowledge has robbed modern man of his dignity and humanity. We worship fact and surety in a world which is uncertain and paradoxical. Rationality cannot be a substitute for wisdom, and Dahlberg feels there is more wisdom in the ancient myths than in all the cold, accumulated facts of modern science.

The unifying metaphor of this section is a comparison of the past to an age of wood and of the present to an age of iron. "There was no iron in Eden," Dahlberg writes, implying that all of man's woes may be traced to the introduction of the material of which machines are made. "Iron appears in Jeremiah, Job and Daniel, the scriptures of weariness . . ." but "Wood was savoury in bucolic Zion" (69). Such an oversimplification of the complexity of the causative factors of modern man's problems may irritate some readers, but it should be underscored that Dahlberg is writing metaphorically, almost as if to illustrate his point: he is using symbols in place of the data that he is so critical of. Iron, in this context, is an appropriate symbol for the cold sterility he sees as characteristic of a modern, mechanized society. Out of iron, man fashions his sophisticated weaponry and complicated machines which lead to mass destruction and mass separation. Wood, on the other hand, though occasionally misused, is more often employed in handicrafts, in domestic tools, and in generally more tranquil and beneficent enterprises.

But Dahlberg is no Romantic primitivist. He does not glorify a "noble savage" living close to nature and uncorrupted by the harassments and confusion of modern civilization. What he laments is the substitution of a heartless rationality for warm, human wisdom and the passing of myth and legend in an overly mechanized world that has lost sight of human needs. "Reason," he tells us, "that does not suckle on proverbs and racial images, which are the vine in the blood, bears the grapes of Sodom" (86). More proverbially, his attack on the futility of modern rationalism is stated succinctly in the aphorism, "Legends tutor the spirit and quiet the race, but metaphysics wears away the mind" (87).

The aphoristic mode of much of *The Flea of Sodom* is testimony to Dahlberg's desire to revive the proverb as a viable genre for the modern age. The aphorism or proverb enables the writer to penetrate into the heart of a matter without recourse to elaborate philosophical doctrine. Philosophy, Dahlberg feels, is tedium; literature, when infused with parable and legend, in the proverbial mode, can lead man to wisdom. The epigram was an important genre to Classical writers because it enabled them to reveal universal truths concisely and with a sense of decorum. Given his extensive Classical background, it is not surprising that the aphorism appeals to Dahlberg's literary temperament. The danger of the form is, of course, that it tends to didactic oversimplification of complex and profound human problems. This simplication disturbs some of his readers, who feel that universal truth is not so easily arrived at. But *The Flea of Sodom* contains only the germs of Dahlberg's experimentation with the genre. The tour de force of Dahlberg's proverbial mode is a later work, *Reasons of the Heart.*

The attack on modernism is continued in "The Wheel of Sheol," Part III of *The Flea of Sodom.* In a legend concerning Beliar's (William Carlos Williams suggests the name is a composite of "Be-" "Liar," and certainly Milton's diabolical Belial is suggested)[11] vision and his fascination with the sacred wheels of Elisha's burning chariot, Dahlberg presents a parable of modern man, fascinated by knowledge which is denied him, and desperate in his attempt to unlock the secrets of the universe. But the wheel, as a symbol of human "progress" (Dahlberg would consider it retrogression), can never satiate man; it drives him to further and further knowledge until all is lost in a babel of confusion. "Beliar was drunk for more iron and gold and more Wheels" (104), just as man hungers after more machines, more materialistic comfort, and more scientific knowledge. But soon the pursuit itself becomes a sickness, drawing man apart from his fellows in a mad quest for scientific fact and material success. For Dahlberg, "Beliar is sick, idiot matter in motion" (105); and, like the wheel, he travels in a continuing circle in a futile and fruitless search.

Ultimately, Beliar cries out for human companionship and rages against time, which is the eternal tragedy of man's lot. He seeks advice from a seer who offers what is Dahlberg's prescription for modern man: "Three things you should heed and do: return to the world, but as a timorous stranger with a precept in his mouth; second, be as nimble as a gazelle to run to a proverb, and as fierce as the lion to devour its meaning; and third, know that forgetting is the depravity of sloth" (110). What man must not forget are the myths and legends which nurtured his race. Instead of a demonic, senseless pursuit of progress, he must stop to discover his roots so that he may better know himself.

In the short section "Bellerophon," Dahlberg summarizes what he has attempted in *The Flea of Sodom;* and he presents his conception of the role of the artist and the function of his art. The primary responsibility of the writer is to write books which alter the lives of his readers: "If a poem does not make the spirit shake as the reed in the wind, it is for infidel unfaith . . ." (113). To be affecting, writers must seek new forms rather than search for something original to say. A thorough Classicist, Dahlberg would agree that great literature is indeed made up of "what oft was said, but ne'er so well exprest." In *The Flea of Sodom* he has attempted to create a new genre by infusing novelistic techniques with mythological allusion and by demonstrating the applicability of ancient legends to contemporary life. As he tells us in the author's note which prefaces the volume, "If this little book appears opaque, the reason is easy to know: the line is gnomic, pulsing with Ovid, Livy, Strabo, Suetonius, Herodian, Plutarch, the Book of Enoch, the Apocalypse of Baruch" (12).

*The Flea of Sodom* does indeed often "appear opaque," but it seems to me less successful than Dahlberg's later experimentation in a somewhat similar mode (*The Sorrows of Priapus*) for other reasons. I have suggested that the book lacks unity or continuity, but more than this factor, the forced and unnatural quality of the allusions throughout tempers its effectiveness. They often seem tacked on to the central narrative, rather than a spontaneous outgrowth of the style. William Carlos Williams, who considered the book a major achievement, nonetheless concluded that "the whole book is subhuman, unintelligible—refusing to be human, refusing to acknowledge analysis."[12] Williams regards these as favorable qualities, for they suggest that Dahlberg is also "refusing to compromise with man as he has become."[13] But they also make it nearly impossible for the reader to react either emotionally or rationally to the work. In response to a question about the use of myth in his writing, Dahlberg remarked: "If the emotion is natural and unaffected, they [the readers] may pass over the myth and still respond to the book, I hope, as natural human beings."[14] This natural response that Dahlberg seeks is not elicited by *The Flea of Sodom.* In its own way, it is a pioneering work in Dahlberg's development because it enabled him to experiment with a richly resonant style that was to become the hallmark of his later work.

CHAPTER 5

# Dionysian Man

THOUGH published over a decade apart, *The Sorrows of Priapus* and *The Carnal Myth* were written as a single work in the late 1950's. Dahlberg explains the genesis of both books (he calls them "satirical erotica") in the introduction to *The Carnal Myth.* The completed manuscript of *The Sorrows of Priapus* was submitted to James Laughlin of New Directions at the suggestion of Sir Herbert Read, for Laughlin had already published *The Flea of Sodom* for which Read had written an introduction. When Laughlin agreed to publish half of the manuscript in an edition illustrated by the well-known American artist, Ben Shahn, Dahlberg was asked to select the chapters to be included from the total manuscript. This done, *The Sorrows of Priapus* appeared in 1957 in two editions—"a chic, fifty dollar edition . . . as well as copies for the commoners." [1] Parts of the remainder of the manuscript appeared in various periodicals as well as in New Directions Annuals, until they were finally assembled by Weybright and Talley in 1968 and published as *The Carnal Myth.* Thus, although this chapter violates the chronological sequence of Dahlberg's work, it seems appropriate to discuss these two books together since they are, in essence, a single work.

## I The Sorrows of Priapus

In a headnote to *The Sorrows of Priapus,* Dahlberg warns his audience that it is "a book for brave readers and poets";[2] and his description is well borne out in the pages that follow. The richly allusive mythologically oriented style, which first made its appearance in *Do These Bones Live* and which was developed in *The Flea of Sodom,* is here even more extensively utilized; and *The Sorrows* is a book which requires a great deal from its readers.

The theme of the work is reflected in the title. Priapus is the god of male generative power in Classical antiquity—the ancient diety of copulation, son of Aphrodite and Dionysus. His sorrows are one with the sorrows of man, who is continually thwarted by his sensuality in his attempt to achieve the "higher life." The carnal nature of man makes him one with the animals; and, though his mind raises him above them, he cannot totally abandon his essentially bestial nature. The central point of *The Sorrows* is concisely expressed by Dahlberg himself in an aphorism from the collection, *Reasons of the Heart:* "What man's head would do is always defeated by his scrotum." [3]

This theme is revealed in the context of myth and fable which support its universality. "Greek worship was a theology of bawds" (3), Dahlberg writes in the Prologue; and his citations and allusions throughout *The Sorrows* are functional rather than mere literary embellishments. They are designed to corroborate the universality of man's carnal nature without groveling in it (as did the literary Naturalists) by encasing it in myth and legend. He begins with an archaic though striking invocation to Venus and presents a catalogue of myths and Classical names which immediately reflect the tone characteristic of Dahlberg's allusive style: "List the courtesans as Homer catalogues the ships at windy Ilium: Chrysis, Corone, Ischas, and Antycra, who quelled many Argives, and relieved Pericles, Aristotle, Aristippus and Sophocles; let them be recollected, and savored once more, and thrice again as an ox's chine" (1).

A meticulous reader, determined to trace every allusion he comes across to its source, will already throw up his hands in despair. One less concerned with authenticity and fact, however, might well pass over the myth (as Dahlberg himself has suggested)[4] as an intrinsic part of the musical, poetic style of *The Sorrows* and appreciate it as such. Though I have suggested that the style is functional, a search for its sources need not blind us to its esthetic merits. In a recent essay on *The Sorrows of Priapus,* Joseph Evans Slate calls it "Edward Dahlberg's Moral Book of Erotic Beasts" and labels the work generically as a bestiary.[5] Certainly the analogues Dahlberg finds between the human condition and the remainder of the animal world substantiate Professor Slate's classification. But the bestial nature of man is only half the story of *The Sorrows;* the other half is the rationality of man which is always in conflict with his animal nature. Man, says Dahlberg, is ruined by "his mind and his pudendum" (10).

In the first chapter of the book, Dahlberg makes extensive comparisons between the sexual habits of man and those of other animals, usually to the detriment of man:

> Whether man is more lecherous than the partridge is doubtful, but he is not as chaste as the raven, who bleeds from the eyes during coition. The man of sensibility is not satisfied with ordinary coupling; all the arts of Lais of Corinth cannot furnish his skin and veins with the infinite sensations he demands. . . . He is almost the only animal that cohabits at all times. With the exception of the pigeon, a bird which abstains only a few days in the year, man has the most lickerish tail of all beasts. This has made him very unruly, and double in his words and deeds. Unlike the elephant he has no seasons for his venery. This pachyderm, after impregnating the female, avoids this excitement for two years. (11)

This "un-natural natural history" reminds us of the Elizabethans who made elaborate comparisons between man and beast one of the hallmarks of the euphuistic prose style. Also reminiscent of the Elizabethan temper are Dahlberg's extensive remarks on man's physiognomy in Chapter II which may enrage the scientifically inclined, but they provide much of the book's humor. "The reason that the tongue is hidden in the mouth," Dahlberg writes with considerable assurance, "is that it can hardly be proud of its vile labors" (27).

Each of man's bodily parts is described and classified in a similar way; but, in keeping with the central theme of *The Sorrows,* Dahlberg's choicest description is reserved for the genital organs: "The phallus is a slovenly bag created without intellect or ontological purpose or design, and as long as the human being has this hanging worm appended to his middle, which is no good for anything except passing urine and getting a few, miserable irritations, for which he forsakes his mother, his father, and his friends, he will never comprehend the Cosmos" (27). This statement may also serve as a concise summary of the entire book.

Though man's sexuality is his animal inheritance, Dahlberg focuses, as I have noted, on the differences between man's carnal nature and the animal's. Man is the only animal which surrounds the sex act with shame and taboo. In most animals, sexual intercourse is as natural an act as breathing; but the more civilized man becomes, the more he represses his natural desires only to create neuroses and unrest. Whether or not this thesis is derived from Freud's *Civilization and its Discontents* we cannot know, but Dahlberg and Freud are in agreement concerning this aspect of civilization's woes. Unhampered by the complexities of civilization, man in his natural state is a good deal more likely to find contentment. "Savages and birds are kinsmen," Dahlberg writes; and he suggests that man can learn a great deal by observing the natural behavior of animals: "There is as much to be learned from a plover, sheldrake, or an eider as from Socrates or the *Laws* of Plato" (40).

Man also might learn a great deal from the animals about choosing his environment with more care. Dahlberg finds urban life particularly hostile to human existence because it separates man from any kind of natural surroundings. Because of this removal from nature, modern man has little sense of place. His cities are masses of steel and concrete with little individuality. Man remains a perpetual wanderer in search of internal peace and stability, but he can rarely find contentment in any of his modern environments. "Men," argues Dahlberg, "show the smallest sense in choosing the earth they wish to sow or a suitable climate" (34). The result is that man and his environment are usually hostile to each other; and, the more urban we become, the more this hostility increases.

The insatiability of the human appetite is the subject of Chapter IV, in which "appetite" is used in the broadest sense of the word, connoting the sum of human needs. "Man's cruelest enemy is his appetite which makes him envious, inconstant, hostile" (43). To illustrate his point, Dahlberg offers a lengthy catalogue of foods and wines which are indicative of man's insatiability. He sees our craving for foods as clearly related to our sexuality, and he suggests that we stuff ourselves with food as a substitute for sexual activity. Again, this view will come as no surprise to readers of Freud, but the difference is that Dahlberg reveals these attributes through myth rather than scientific research and that he makes extensive use of the un-natural, natural history which I have already noted. Imagine a scientist's reaction to the following lines: "Oysters are aphrodisiacs, and the dolphin is fierce, and it is possible that those that devour them acquire their traits" (46). This kind of remark has led at least one critic to comment upon

Dahlberg's *faux naïveté*,[6] but I believe that he takes the factual substance of Dahlberg's remarks a bit too seriously. Certainly these metaphorical comments lack scientific basis, but they do serve to illustrate Dahlberg's contention in this chapter that "Man can never attain . . . vision . . . so long as he is incontinent, overeats, and is covetous" (47).

Dahlberg's account of man's origins in Chapter V of *The Sorrows of Priapus* is in keeping with this antiscientific approach, and factually oriented literalists find little manna in it. The truths of man's beginnings, Dahlberg feels, are more meaningfully recorded in myth and fable than in scientific speculation: Hesiod is a surer guide to our ultimate nature than is Darwin. In Renaissance fashion, Dahlberg sees man as an intermediate form between angel and beast. Midway on the Great Chain of Being, man is pulled in both directions, his intellect raising him toward the angels, his carnality limiting his potential. "Man is at present in a misshapen stage, neither possessing the gentler customs of the beast, nor the faculties of the angel" (54). Because of the ingenuity with which man has continually attempted to explain his origins, the chapter also contains some of the more humorous passages in the book: "Aristophanes claimed that there were at first three sexes, man, woman, and man-woman. This creature was round and he had eight limbs; his back and sides were a circle, and he had two faces. The monster had four ears and two privy members, and he rolled everywhere. He had no need to couple with another because he was altogether self-sufficient, although it is hard to understand how he connected his two parts" (50).

Re-emphasizing the duality of human nature, Dahlberg concludes the first section of *The Sorrows*. Thematically, the first five chapters are the most unified section of the work, for each focuses upon the relationship of man to the natural world. Section II, entitled "The Myth Gatherers," though occasionally concerned with man's carnality, deals more explicitly with pre-Columbian legends and with the exploration of the New World. Reminiscent of *In the American Grain* by William Carlos Williams (to whom the section is dedicated), "The Myth Gatherers" is an attempt to equate the myths of the New World with those of Classical antiquity in order to underscore the universality of the mythological impulse in man.

For Dahlberg, the exploration of the New World was a search

for a new energy. Like Henry Adams, he senses man's deeply rooted need for unity. The New World provided an outlet for man's explorative appetite, and it quickly revealed itself as a fertile seedbed of myth. The centuries of inhabitation by primitive cultures had created a legendary past, one totally alien to the European experience but one with surprising parallels. Our systematic destruction of the Indian way of life has made this legendary past almost inaccessible to us since the creation of myth is related to the land; and, as we ravaged the land, we removed the rituals associated with it. "We have lost the ground, city-cursed that we are, left it behind us like the *Quiche* did the *Yaqui* for whom they wept" (63).

Chapter VII of *The Sorrows of Priapus* reverts to the earlier theme of the work, beginning with the statement, "All the errors concerning the human race come from not realizing that man is another animal" (65). Dahlberg quickly, however, modifies this essentially Naturalistic position by suggesting that man's awareness of his past enables him to temper his animality, though he can never totally transcend it. This awareness of the past is ritualized in legend and myth; and, even in his most primitive state, man has not ignored the need for fable to explain, justify, and make purposeful his life. These pre-Columbian legends demonstrate that man seeks wisdom by thirsting after the absolute, even in his least civilized condition.

Thus the following four chapters (VIII-XI) are attempts to rediscover the legends of the redman in order to make us aware of the cultural heritage which we have suppressed. Dahlberg points out many relationships between the pre-Columbian experience, Classical mythology, and religious ritual. "Montezuma," he tells us, "was as much given to copal and the perfume of flowers as King Midas, who, after debauching his realm, offered Zeus his father's farm wagon" (74). After a description of the Mexican goddess, Tlacotteutl, who, according to Dahlberg, represents "human perversity," he cites St. Paul who "relates in the *Epistle to the Romans* that whatever he resolved to do, he seldom did" (78–79). Discussing the universal fear of deformity, Dahlberg compares Inca ritual with Hebraic custom: "The Inca banished the deformed from holy places save on certain feasts; the blind, the one-handed could not enter the temple of Jerusalem. . . . The sacrificial animal of the Inca and the Israelite was without defect" (84).

This comparative method emphasizes the striking similarities between man's continuing attempts to reconstruct his origins, and it suggests a continuum in human nature which bears little relationship to the kind of civilization men have constructed.

In these chapters, Dahlberg examines in detail the legends of the Aztecs, the Incas, the Mayans, and the Quiche-Mayan peoples; and he finds their colorful legends, explaining universal mysteries, more meaningful than a host of scientific tracts. For when man encases his search for absolute truth in a mythological framework, he is able to maintain his sanity and sense of purpose. When he makes this search a scientific investigation based upon fact and statistics, the impossibility of it becomes clear, and he is driven to madness and irrationality. Like Manco Capac, the Inca ruler who brought civilization to his people but became insane when he attempted to discover the *Pachacamac* or "universe quickener," man must realize his limitations or he will be driven over the precipice of rationality. "Were it not that man is irrational either in the beginning or at the close of his life," Dahlberg writes, "Manco Capac would have been a god" (86).

The final section of *The Sorrows of Priapus* is a discussion of the topography of the North American continent, with particular attention given to the rivers, plants, and trees of the New World. The river, here as elsewhere in Dahlberg's writing, serves as a functional symbol representing the flow and continuity of life. When he writes that "Our annals are weak, and we know not our rivers" (106), he surely means it in both a literal and a figurative sense: we know not from where we came nor where we are going. The river serves also as a connective for the world's legends: "Nations are children everywhere, and the rituals in all countries are very much the same, for they are tributary rivers of one great parent stream, Ocean, the father of Earth" (110). Representative also of that which binds men together, Dahlberg's catalogues of rivers are natural symbols of his search for human identity.

A chapter on the vegetative growth of the New World concludes the book with a similarly symbolic note. Like rivers, plants also function symbolically in terms of man's search for his roots and his connection to the earth. "Unrelated to the desert, the rivers, the forests, man is feeble and a random fornicator" (117). To know ourselves, Dahlberg insists again and again, we must remain attached to the earth which has given us life. The last paragraph of *The Sorrows of Priapus* is as explicit a statement of what we might term Dahlberg's "cultured primitivism" as can be found anywhere in his work. Tempered by his inherent classicism and attachment to myth, it is a plea to return to a simplified life, close to nature and away from the complex inhumanity of modern urban civilization: "Where are the little hills which shall bring justice, or the fruits of Lebanon? O forest spectre, ferns, lichens, boleti contain Eden. Be primordial or decay" (119).

Josephine Herbst has very accurately noted that the key word here is "justice." "Justice," she writes, "is not native to the primordial world but belongs to the human."[7] Dahlberg is no René Chateaubriand exalting the "noble savage" and urging us to leave our "civilized" ways behind us. What disturbs him is not only what has become of our civilization, but how it has corrupted our humanity. Dahlberg may send us to the woods, but he surely wants us to take our books with us.

In sum, *The Sorrows of Priapus* is an unusual book which fits none of our traditional generic classifications. As pointed out by Professor Slate, it contains elements of the bestiary; but it is also something of a travel book, a geographical handbook, a collection of myths and fables, and an essay on human nature. Were it more scientifically oriented, we might call it an anthropological study which demonstrates man's relationship to the animal world, or a study in ecology which deals with interrelationships between man and his environment. But then, too, it is a critique of science and the scientific method. For fact and statistic, Dahlberg substitutes myth and ritual; and, like the earlier *Flea of Sodom,* it has a literary form of its own—one that is distinctly Dahlberg's, but one that is also a fusion of many traditional genres.

## II The Carnal Myth

The introduction to *The Carnal Myth* contains a detailed statement of Dahlberg's literary credo, a description of the evolution of the work, and an off-hand attack on contemporary academic critics. Repeating a familiar complaint, Dahlberg bemoans the fact that a truthful writer—one who refuses to compromise his art—is doomed to neglect and abuse. In case there is any uncertainty as to whom these remarks are about, he notes "Since my prentice to letters, I have belonged to the sodality of one" (3). The acerbic tone of Dahlberg's remarks are evidence of the misanthropic temper which characterizes much of his later writing. It is indeed paradoxical that a writer who is most accurately labeled a humanist should speak with such bitterness about his fellow man, but the paradox is perhaps best explained by what Dahlberg feels is a continuing neglect of his work and by the exaltation by "criticasters," as he calls our academic critics of lesser writers. When notified of his inclusion on the list of "Ten most neglected American writers" published in *Book World,* Dahlberg remarked, "Of the ten writers on this list, nine deserve to be neglected." [8] Such blustery arrogance is not calculated to endear him to many, and it is the reason why Dahlberg has had so much difficulty forming lasting friendships.

Describing the origins of *The Carnal Myth* in this introduction, Dahlberg relates his discovery in 1951 of a large body of pre-Columbian myths which he felt had as much significance for modern man as Grecian or Roman legends. As he stated in *The Sorrows of Priapus,* "Let no one assume that the fables of the red races of the three Americas do not invigorate the intellect" (66). Thus he began a study of early native American legend and history, taking note of parallels between these materials and Classical literature. The result was a rather lengthy study in comparative mythology. I have already discussed the genesis of Dahlberg's completed manuscript—the first part published as *The Sorrows of Priapus,* and the second, a decade later, as *The Carnal Myth.*

*The Carnal Myth* very quickly reveals itself as a part of the earlier work. The book begins with a critique of the lack of discretion men display in their choice of a mate or sexual partner. Sexual desire, it is suggested, blinds men to all significant considerations and causes them to behave animalistically: "The majority of persons choose their wives with as little prudence as they eat. They see a trull with nothing else to recommend her but a pair of thighs and choice hunkers, and so smart to void their seed that they marry her at once" (13). Man may become more intellectually sophisticated, but he retains his essential bestiality because it is impossible for him to transcend it. In Dahlberg's words, "man cannot be seraphic until nature has altered his body" (22). This chapter of *The Carnal Myth* seems closely related to the third chapter of *The Sorrows of Priapus,* emphasizing as it does the conflict between man's aspirations and his limitations, between his civilized nature and his animal nature. When we recall that both books were originally part of a single manuscript, it is indeed possible that these chapters were together in the initial conception.

If man's sensuality is his most universal attribute, his inclination to violence is not very far behind. "Mars and Venus are the two pests of humanity" (24), Dahlberg writes. The Classical writers, he reminds us, could hardly write about man other than in battle because conflict is the fable of human behavior. Again echoing Freud, Dahlberg suggests that war often serves as a substitute for sexuality: "Alexander was indifferent to women; Babylon, Arabia, Palestine, India, Africa were his meal" (33). This inclination to violence is the most difficult human attribute to understand, primarily because it can never be satisfied. A sense of physical gratification may explain the sex drive, but man's penchant for violence is insatiable and thoroughly irrational: "Men may waste away for the favors of women, which at least is a logical greed, but no one can fill his gullet with several seas and continents or has the human strength to walk once around a domain that includes Asia and Europe" (33).

Chapters III and IV of *The Carnal Myth* discuss the problem of aging and its impact upon human behavior. One of the primary human fears is that of growing old, of losing youthful vigor and energy. Again comparing man to the animals, Dahlberg finds homo sapiens much more submissive to death than most animals. Man dies senile and goes out with a proverbial whimper. This lessens the quality of his life because death is a negation of energy, and man must rage against it. Dahlberg suggests that we imitate the elephants: "Melancholy or distempered elephants tear up grass, which refreshes the soul far more than the pellets of Aesculapius, which makes cowards of whole races. It is good to die casting up grass toward heaven, and he who is wise will accept his fate with the anger of a pachyderm, for it is best to die in battle" (52). Paradoxically, Dahlberg remarks a paragraph later that "It is idle and insane to complain against nature" (52). How man can rage against death without complaining against nature is difficult to comprehend.

A lengthy digression from the main subject of *The Carnal Myth* in Chapter V contains the most extensive discussion of the art of writing to be found in Dahlberg's works. He begins by making several observations about writers: they are difficult to know or become close with; they are rarely gregarious because their profession is by its nature a lonely one. Reminiscent of his comments on nineteenth-century American writers in *Can These Bones Live,* he intimates that writing, because of its solitary nature, separates men from each other and works against the formation of meaningful and deep human relationships. Dahlberg again attacks current literature and reminds us of the superiority of the ancient writers. Never fearing hyperbole, he cites La Fontaine who "believed that anyone who preferred his own time to that of the ancients was insane" (61). Great writing must be constantly rediscovered because nothing "new" really emerges from literature.

Again echoing *Can These Bones Live,* he argues that our preoccupation with originality is the curse of the modern world. Instead of being slavishly devoted to the proposition that to be original is to be a great writer, our authors should strive to write books that reflect their humanity and individuality. We have produced too many "cold" books which are divorced from human concerns; and, if we are to discover the most elemental of these concerns, we must turn to our mythological heritage. Because writers, particularly poets, are the "guardians of the race," they must seek to preserve their cultural heritage by re-examining the legendary traditions of their people. They must remain uncommitted to dogmas, particularly to those of their own time which would alienate them from their meaningful past. Our greatest writers were not great innovators, but artists who were able to use the past successfully, in terms of the lessons it provides for their own times.

In this sense, they were essentially moralists whose concerns were ethical rather than esthetic. Another of the plagues of modernity is that we are too much devoted to esthetics and not enough to morality. Dahlberg agrees with Plato who suggested that music "enslaved the multitude," and he urges us to pay more attention to thought than to form. Clearly this "poetics" is a reflection of Dahlberg's own particular mode of writing, but it would be a mistake to prescribe it too widely. Moreover, where would Dahlberg himself be if we all turned away from the moderns to read the Classics? But the dispute here outlined is developed in much more detail in *Truth Is More Sacred,* a book which Dahlberg co-authored with Sir Herbert Read which revives the Battle of the Books for our own time.

Returning to the more central aspect of the book in Chapter VI,

Dahlberg reminds us that it is impossible for men to exercise restraint in sexual matters because sex dominates human activity. Paradoxically, however, man needs peace, quiet, and rest although his libido makes these difficult to attain. "Everybody has to choose, and one will honor neither a man who abstains from a lust of which he has no knowledge nor a teacher who feigns that pleasure does not exist" (71). Consistent with his humanism, Dahlberg again argues for a *media via* between asceticism and lechery. We must be cognizant of man's carnal nature, but there is no need to grovel in it.

The remainder of *The Carnal Myth* is a restatement of ideas and themes initially introduced in *The Sorrows of Priapus.* Dahlberg re-emphasizes the need for human companionship which men so rarely satisfy. He argues that men are often disappointed by friends because self-interest usually conquers the desire to pursue mutual interests, and the latter is central to any lasting friendship. He again comments upon the American desertion of nature; and, in a phrase which foreshadows the title of *The Leafless American,* a recent collection of his essays, Dahlberg tells us that "The American is a treeless ghost" (84). As in *The Sorrows of Priapus,* he sees a need for man to remain close to his geographical origins if he is to understand his roots. He must not desert the plenitude of nature for the sterility and barrenness of the city.

The concluding chapters are another extended analysis of early exploration of the New World, and they clearly belong with the "Myth Gatherers" section of *The Sorrows of Priapus.* Reiterating the idea that the explorative urge in man is a search for his origins, Dahlberg examines the search for the Seven Cities of Cibola and the explorations of de Soto, Magellan, and Jacques Cartier. These myth gatherers sought a golden age of the past; they were seekers after our legendary origins; and we need to recapture the spirit of their ventures. "[T]he American is far from the Indian god rivers, bays, rain, and maize that give him images, without which he is sourceless. Until he is connected with the fens, the ravines, the stars, he is more solitary than any beast. Man is a god, and kin to men, when he is a river, a mountain, a horse, a moon" (97). Our legends, our myths, our rituals, our fables *create* our humanity. They are the *differentiae* between man and the remainder of the animal world.

While these chapters contain some of Dahlberg's most poetic

prose (as illustrated by the passage just quoted), they are also indicative of the major weakness of *The Carnal Myth*: its repetitiveness. Almost all the ideas and themes developed in it had already been dealt with at length in the earlier volume. The endless catalogues of rivers, trees, and other geographical features is more effective initially; but it grows somewhat tiresome when carried on long after the central point has been made. Sometimes, though clearly not so often as in *The Flea of Sodom*, the prose seems an exercise in name dropping; and the relationship between citation and subject matter is somewhat tenuous.[9]

Taken together, *The Sorrows of Priapus* and *The Carnal Myth* are an experiment in genre which provides a dazzling exhibition of Dahlberg's style. Thematically, the major thrust of both works is indicated in their titles: man's bestiality and his sensuality limit his potential and always thwart his intellect. His dualistic nature has been the main concern of myth and legend, and this concern is reflected in native American Indian myth as well as in Classical mythology. Secondary themes in both works are the search for human origins, man's need to relate closely to nature, and the sterility of modern civilization.

Both books are indeed for "brave readers," as Dahlberg remarks in the headnote to *The Sorrows of Priapus*. They require an intense response which involves the reader directly in searching out subject and theme from style and rhetoric. Medium and message in these works are often separable, but the tendency is to exalt the former at the expense of the latter. For, when removed from the baroque splendor of Dahlberg's style, the ideas expressed may seem to some readers overly simplistic or naïve. But surely Dahlberg is not simply suggesting that reading the Classics and returning to nature will solve all of the world's ills. What he is attempting to do in these works, as he writes in a letter to Karl Shapiro, is "to provide an indigenous myth for the poet." [10] As such, they are sourcebooks of our native heritage and recover a good deal of our "usable past" for us.

CHAPTER 6

# Vain Scribblers

CAN *These Bones Live* includes some commentary concerning contemporary literature (notably on Hemingway, Faulkner and the proletarian writers); and Dahlberg's attitude toward modern writers may be generally garnered from *The Sorrows of Priapus* and *The Carnal Myth.* However, his most extended discussion of modern letters occurs in *Truth Is More Sacred,* a book he co-authored with Sir Herbert Read. This work and *Alms for Oblivion,* a memoir which contains a good deal of incidental criticism, are in essence an attack on modernism; and they contain caustic condemnations of writers whom we have canonized as the literary saints of our century. Considering the iconoclastic nature of Dahlberg's opinions, it is surprising that neither work has gained widespread attention. For despite the fact that his judgments may strike some readers as dense and biased, his arguments are always provocative; and, whether or not they alter our well-conditioned opinions, his essentially moralistic approach may serve as a corrective to the esthetically oriented critical temper of our day.

## I Truth Is More Sacred

If we had more books like *Truth Is More Sacred* the state of contemporary literary criticism would be much healthier than it is. Epistolary exchanges on the state of literature by men of differing literary temperaments have often produced stimulating critical discussions. The Henry James–H. G. Wells letters come immediately to mind, or the Mark Twain–William Dean Howells correspondence. The Read–Dahlberg correspondence engages our interest because it enables us to focus clearly upon two widely divergent approaches to literature and to identify the assumptions embodied in each.

The points of contention between Dahlberg and Read in these letters almost always can be distilled to a rather fundamental dispute between a moralist and an esthetician. Dahlberg's premise is that the function of art is to ennoble man and "elevate" the race. This can only be done by "purifying" the language and by ridding it of the vulgarities of the "garage proletariat." Our age may be diffuse, vulgar, venal, and coarse; but it is certainly not the business of the writer to perpetuate any of these attributes. He must rise above his age by immersing himself in the greatest literature of the past, and he should attempt to model his style on the achievements of the best writers of the tradition in which he writes. Read, while not denying the need for *implicit* morality in art, objects when it becomes the overriding concern of the artist at the expense of esthetic considerations. Writers overly preoccupied with morality tend toward didacticism, and their work very quickly degenerates into self-righteous sermonizing. To avoid this danger, a writer's central concern should be with questions of form, style, structure, and unity—essentially esthetic qualities which contribute to the effect he wishes his art to elicit.

These two approaches are as old as criticism itself, and it is not likely that we will ever see them resolved—nor would we want to. For together they broaden our perspective of a literary work and increase our understanding of it. As David Daiches indicates, "Every effective literary critic sees some facet of literary art and develops our awareness with respect to it; but the total vision, or something approximating it, comes only to those who learn how to blend the insights yielded by many critical approaches." [1] Thus, we can learn a good deal from both Dahlberg and Read, and it seems less useful to condemn either the moralist or the esthetic position than to understand the terms of their conflict in order to sharpen our own critical faculties.

The title of the Dahlberg–Read correspondence comes from a quotation attributed to Socrates alluded to by Dahlberg in a letter to Read about Eliot and Pound: "You told me in New York that T. S. Eliot had been a friend of yours for above forty years. Now before you defend this *mungrell* versifier I must needs cite Sokrates who asserted that truth is more sacred than friendship." [2] Such a remark sounds foreign coming from Dahlberg because it counters the premise of much of his earlier criticism which places human relationships above devotion to abstract ideals. Read, noting the inconsistency, replies: "One of the most melancholy aspects of our time has been the ease with which men have sacrificed their friends for some 'truth,' religious or political. I have no intention of doing that, on this or any other occasion" (209). The discrepancy arises, we feel, because Dahlberg refers to "truth" in the singular as an absolute quality, while Read speaks of "some truth" as a relativist and reflects more accurately the prevailing tendency of our time. We might strike a balance by suggesting that "truth"—if, indeed, we can ever discover it—*is* more sacred than friendship; but "truths" most assuredly are not.

The writers discussed in the exchange of letters are James Joyce, D. H. Lawrence, Henry James, T. S. Eliot, and Ezra Pound, with a few pages devoted to less formidable figures. Dahlberg's remarks about these writers are almost all negative; Read's, for the most part, positive. Dahlberg would have us re-establish our literary hierarchy in the twentieth century by dethroning those writers we have established as our most important literary figures. Just who he would replace them with is not clear, for his attack is directed at modernism generally; and he culminates with the familiar plea that we return to the Classics and the ancient writers for wisdom and literary nourishment. When Dahlberg dismisses Eliot, Pound, and Joyce (as well as André Gide, Jean Cocteau, Arthur Rimbaud, Paul Verlaine) as "bawds in the beauty parlor on Mount Ida"(12), his antagonism is directed at what he thinks to be the symptoms of decadence in the modern literary temper: the decline of language, the celebration of pedantry, the negation of human values, the flourishing of sham and pretense.

For Dahlberg, James Joyce is perhaps the writer most representative of literary modernism; therefore he begins his part of the correspondence with a critique of Joyce, with most of his ire directed at *Ulysses.* Refusing to mince words or temper judgment, Dahlberg calls Joyce's masterpiece "a twenty-four hours' journey through ordure" and a "novel of epic cowardice"(18). His criticism of the novel emphasizes its preoccupation with that which is base in man without attempting to symbolize the vulgarity being described. "I do not blame him [Joyce] for divulging all the vices of men but for reducing them to unheroic dimensions. We must call wrath, dirt, lust, drunkenness—Agamemnon, Thersites, Ajax, Nestor, or sink the giants into little everyday characters"(18). Certainly this charge seems an odd one to level at Joyce who modeled his novel after a Homeric epic and consistently sought to give it mythic dimensions. But Dahlberg's evaluation does not stop here. He further admonishes Joyce for his "dismemberment" of the language which results in pedantic word play rather than in literary artistry. A literature which moves away from the "human" and substitutes grammar and syntax for feeling and myth is, to Dahlberg, doomed to failure. "Who cares to exhaust his brain searching for a verb which has wandered away from the substantive, or look for a noun that has been abducted by Pluto, or was never born?"(20).

Read's response to Dahlberg's remarks is directed at the moralistic premise of the critique: "You seem to be calling on the poet to purify men's hearts. I would say that that is the business of the priest or the philosopher, and that it is the poet's business to purify their eyes. We cannot feel aright unless we see aright. The whole function of art is cathartic, not didactic"(27). On these grounds he urges Dahlberg to restrain from reviling artists who, Read feels, are the "lightbearers" of our civilization; and he suggests that the criticism contained in these letters be directed at the civilization itself which, because of apathy and dull sensibilities, cannot respond to the beauties of art. "The real enemies of literature," Read argues, "are not our corrupted brothers, but the forces that corrupt them—the whole of the hideous, heartless civilization in which we are involved"(22). He defends *Ulysses* in terms of its intrinsic beauty, while not denying the validity of some of Dahlberg's critique. *Ulysses,* he concedes, may be a sick book; but it well reflects its time and is a penetrating diagnosis of our social ills.

But Dahlberg does not relent. In his next letter he becomes more specific about the "canting, riff-raff English"(35) of *Ulysses,* citing examples along the way. He accuses Joyce of being a mere cataloguer whose "recitation of sundry Dublin thoroughfares is a phlegmatic street-directory. An author does not ennoble the intellect by merely mentioning the sages or myths which are sacred to humanity"(39). When we recall Dahlberg's own extensive use of the catalogue technique, particularly in *The Sorrows of Priapus,* the accusation loses some of its force.

Dahlberg's final letter about Joyce salvages some little virtue from *Ulysses.* He notes that there is one "imperial theme" in the novel—the lament for Ireland's golden age of the past. But as a whole, Dahlberg finds the work "a Gargantuan urinal"(47) which has been overpraised and which has had a baneful effect on our language and literature. Sir Herbert, however, has the final word on Joyce and attempts to arrive at some balanced appraisal. Surprisingly, he agrees that *Ulysses* has been overpraised, and he suggests that Joyce's best writing occurs in his earlier work—*Dubliners* and *Portrait of the Artist as a Young Man.* Read admires the sensitivity and concentration of Joyce's prose, and he reiterates his judgment of *Ulysses* as a novel symptomatic of our time. *Ulysses,* he argues, reflects the "spiritual darkness" and ambiguity of modern man; and, in so doing, it is successful. He agrees that Joyce devotes too much of his art to word play and riddles, but this is most apparent in *Finnegans Wake* which both Dahlberg and Read concur is ineffective and tedious. As Read puts it, "It is the desperate obliquity of a man who can no longer look reality in the face"(64). It is a *monumental* failure to be sure, but a failure nevertheless.

The exchange of letters about D. H. Lawrence is less acerbic, although Read is clearly more sympathetic to Lawrence's achievement than is Dahlberg. The latter retains strong personal feelings about Lawrence—it may be remembered that Lawrence wrote the introduction to *Bottom Dogs*—but he attempts to evaluate Lawrence's literary accomplishments objectively and without nostalgia. "Nostalgia," he writes here, "is a stumbling block to perception"(80). Attempting to avoid that stumbling block, Dahlberg is most critical of Lawrence's diction, what he calls "insipid puerilities" and "droll similes" in Lawrence's style. But, in all, the letters about Lawrence express Dahlberg's most favorable opinion of any of the writers he discusses in *Truth Is More Sacred. Studies in Classic American Literature* Dahlberg cites as Lawrence's best and most important book, a judgment which is not surprising, given its apparent influence on *Can These Bones Live.*

The letters on Henry James are quite another matter. He is dealt with rather harshly, particularly in contrast to the lukewarm praise accorded Lawrence. Dahlberg's opening paragraph on James well reflects the tone and substance of his remarks: "Henry James was as debilitated in his books as Pope was in life; the latter could scarce stand on his feet, while the former, perspiring over his syntax, sends those he tortures to Egyptian ideographic writings in which a pair of legs going denotes the transitive verb"(121). James's preoccupation with sentence construction, form, structure, unity, and so on seem to Dahlberg to remove his writing from the sphere of human feeling and reaction. He finds it impossible to react emotively to James's work because it is overly literary and devoid of passion. This complaint is indeed a familiar one, for it is often leveled at James by nonmembers of the James cult. In this judgment, as in few others in *Truth Is More Sacred,* Dahlberg has many allies.

Read's reaction to James's work is as predictable as Dahlberg's. Always the esthetician, Read admires those very qualities of James's art that Dahlberg despises. He asserts that Dahlberg gives James no credit for creating a viable and intense fictional form, which is as well structured and carefully planned as a Classical drama. Read applauds the architectonics of James's art, its discipline and perfection. He admits that the Jamesian style is idiosyncratic, but reminds us that this is true of almost all of our great prose stylists—Sir Thomas Browne, Laurence Sterne, George Meredith (and, we are tempted to add, Dahlberg himself).

The discussion of James ends inconclusively because Dahlberg and Read approach him from such thoroughly divergent points of view, but the section does contain an excellent summary of Dahlberg's limitations as a critic. Disturbed by what Read feels is Dahlberg's overly dogmatic disparagement of James, he comments: "You are absolute for truth, and like a Grand Inquisitor, would send to the stake any author who in any respect offends your dogma. That dogma is not strictly aesthetic—on the contrary, from the beginning of this correspondence you have spoken of virtue and health. Your conception of the great writer is that of a sage or a seer, a patriarch who instructs his people in a voice of authority, and castigates them with whips of scorn when they are weak and errant" (143).

"Absolute for truth," as Read puts it, Dahlberg often fails to consider the implications of his critical tenets which would, if carried to a logical conclusion, produce a literature that is didactic and almost totally devoid of originality. But then Dahlberg has often written that originality is the curse of modernity. More than this, however, it must strike the objective reader as ironic that those writers who bear the brunt of Dahlberg's scorn—James, Joyce, Eliot, and Pound—are in one sense the writers who have promulgated the same literary values which Dahlberg holds dear. Who has more forcefully argued for a continuity of literary tradition than Eliot? What writer's work reflects as thorough a familiarity with the Classics as does Joyce's? And, finally, who was more concerned with the shaping of literary style than was Henry James? Each of these qualities is an intrinsic part of Dahlberg's literary consciousness, but he is unable to appreciate them in other writers.

After a considerable attack on Robert Graves, a writer who seems curiously out of place in this collection,[3] Dahlberg takes on Eliot and Pound, accusing them, among other things, of plagiarism, anti-Semitism, and corruption of the English language. The charge about plagiarism is somewhat ironic coming from Dahlberg as he has so often argued that originality is a fetish and has urged writers not to fear imitating and borrowing from the Classics. Even Josephine Herbst, one of Dahlberg's most sympathetic critics, finds the accusation astonishing: "in view of Dahlberg's profuse use of learned citations, however otherwise employed, this is an astounding malediction."[4] The charge of anti-Semitism is more substantial, and it has often been made against Eliot and Pound. The third point—the corruption of the language—is more closely related to Dahlberg's concept of the function of literature and is consistent with his position throughout his works.

Dahlberg himself regards this offense as the most serious one. He is willing to ignore the plagiarism; pass over the anti-Semitism, "ignominious as it is"; but he cannot forgive them for destroying "the sacred fables of diction." He makes the charge in a burst of pulpit oratory worthy of a Cotton Mather: "I accuse these men of having betrayed the trust bequeathed to them by Homer, Hesiod, Horace, Theognis, Heraclitus, Propertius, Martial, Aristotle, Chaucer, Fletcher, John Webster and Shakespeare. I charge them, along with their dead myrmidons, James Joyce and Wyndham Lewis, with having broken the Ten Commandments of the English language" (173). For Dahlberg, the degradation of language is symptomatic of the degradation of man. When we attempt to refine our language and to elevate it above the commonalities of everyday diction, we have taken a large step toward achieving a higher level of civilization. Thus those writers who seek to bring the "vulgarities of the crowd" into our literature are, according to Dahlberg, the enemies of culture rather than its proponents. They must be exposed at all costs.

This argument is a rather tenuous one and we have the feeling that Dahlberg protests a bit too much. The question of whether or not the language spoken by the masses should be the same as the language of literature is an ancient one that is seemingly impossible to resolve. We cannot know whether Homer wrote in the *patois* of his day, but certainly Chaucer can as easily be condemned for using the language of the streets ("But with his mouth he kiste hir naked ers") as can T. S. Eliot. Dahlberg's conclusion that Eliot and Pound have "set back literature a hundred years" seems a bit excessive, and by contrast Sir Herbert's more tempered defense of their poetry gains our sympathy.

The Dahlberg–Read correspondence aroused some hostile feelings between the two men, though they remained friends for many years. When I asked Dahlberg about the experience of writing *Truth Is More Sacred,* he outlined the origins and genesis of the work in the following letter, which I include nearly in its entirety since it is unavailable elsewhere:

> Now, I must perforce tell you a little of the origins of the book Sir Herbert and I wrote together. I was in London at the time, and told my dear, now deceased friend, that it was time a truthful book about modern literature should be written, and that I was sick unto death of all the mouldy tomes scribbled about Eliot, Pound, Joyce, and James. We had walked through Russell Square in London, and I said that no one with probity or a tittle of taste would ever title a play of his: The Cocktail Party. Sir Herbert agreed, and said he now had misgivings about Eliot, and he also remarked that Eliot was no considerable reader.
>
> Then at the Audeley Pub we engaged in an earnest discussion about a book we might write together. I said that Pound was a mountebank and that we ought to include Graves, only because of his immense influence upon fifty years of readers and prentice authors. But Read objected, saying that Graves was not worth our time. I insisted, though I agreed that Graves was an outrageous plagiary (all my proof was excised because the legal advisor to Horizon Press said that Graves could sue); well the truth is libel nowadays.
>
> First, we approached, or rather he did, Mrs. Wolfe, of the Pantheon Press, and though a warm adherent of his, she declined, much to the chagrin of Read. Then he asked Ben Raeburn, of Horizon Press about such a book, and Mr. Raeburn, an enthusiast, was quite willing to publish a book of epistolary essays.
>
> Neither Read nor I had any thought of engaging in a personal

battle; he admitted that he would be the devil's advocate of the contemporary writers, and so we commenced the volume. Read also acknowledged that he knew far less about the ancient Greeks than I did. Then for above twenty-five years Read had said in one letter or another that I was his Socratic gadfly and his Conscience, but despite all my exhortations, he made every conceivable concession to the public. Don't ask me who the public is; I don't know, and never give a thought to pleasing one soul when I am making ready to compose a line.

At the beginning of the book everything between my friend and me went along very well. I did my best to explain what real belles lettres is, and he replied, and both of us were quiet and reposeful.

By the time I had reached the Eliot quandary, unlook'd for trouble arose. I sent him the essay, and received, as usual, an affectionate reply, and he wrote that he was not agitated at all by what I had said. Then after some weeks had transpired I received his own chapter calling me a Grand Inquisitor of my contemporaries. So the warfare began, and from then on, it was my wit against his, and what a dearth of that ore there is in our books. Instead of advancing Eliot's cause, he impugned me, and this angered me a great deal. Then, it was Ben Raeburn, who suggested that the title of the book be taken from the citation I had culled from Plato: "Truth is more sacred than friendship," a remark supposed to have been made by Socrates. And Read thought this a fine title, that is, the parcel of the quotation, Truth is more Sacred. Much to my amazement, the man who disclosed that I knew far more about antique Hellas than he, said that I had mutilated the assertion, which is impossible. Aside from that, had I done so, why had he not objected to it at the beginning, instead of saying it was the authentic title of an entire work?

Again, after his insistence that we exclude Graves he praised him!

It took me months to ransack the doggerel of Eliot, and the specious polysyllables of Joyce, and the stammering sentences of Henry James, before I felt I was prepared to compose a single sentence. Read depended upon his memory, a very fragile vessel indeed, and got off his rejoinders in a pair of weeks or less.

That Read never forgave me cannot be misdoubted. After this book no matter how he had lauded me as a prose stylist, he declined to mention me in any book of his. I asked how I could be a great author in one of his Introductions to my work, and not even exist in any of his volumes. He never mentioned it to me. When I suggested that Tolstoi's *What Is Art?* was prophetic de-

> spite certain dogmas about letters I could not accept, he was disdainful. Once more I was later startled to discover that he wrote about *What Is Art?* And no reference to me at all. On another occasion I stated that a common weal of any worth at all depended upon the purity of the language of its poets and writers. He wrote a whole chapter on the purity of English, and cited just about everybody in our alleged Helicon except me.
>
> I broke off relations with Herbert Read, until Laughlin at New Directions told me that Herbert was sorely grieved, and that I should write to him, which I did, and continued to do until his last few, tormenting days. I grieved over his life and suffered when he died. Herbert Read wrote some lovely, bucolic lines in his earliest beginnings, but there was bread to be gotten, and how many have cast their loaves upon the waters, and alas received them. Each man selects his portion, may be disappointed with it afterwards, but it is he who asked for it.

It would be interesting if we had a letter from Read explaining the genesis of the work to place alongside this one, but unfortunately none that I know of exists.

As a whole, *Truth Is More Sacred* reveals Dahlberg's literary criticism at its best and at its worst. His voice may seem to us a cry in the wilderness; but it is a formidable voice, outraged at modernity and calling to task our most revered contemporary authors. If, at times, his rage may blind him to the accomplishments of his peers, it is understandable, given the considerable neglect his own work has suffered. Although some may be unable to condone his continuing invective and considerable arrogance, *Truth Is More Sacred* (at least Dahlberg's half of it) is his well earned shout of defiance.

## II Alms for Oblivion

Unlike the epistolary exchange with Read, *Alms for Oblivion* is divided almost equally between praise and blame of the writers discussed. A gossipy, chatty book, it is again a combination of various Dahlbergian forms and themes. Much of it—indeed, the most successful pages—is memoir. Dahlberg relates his experiences with the expatriates in Paris and his friendship with Sherwood Anderson, Theodore Dreiser, Ford Madox Ford, and many other American writers living abroad. Another part of *Alms for Oblivion* is literary criticism. There are essays on *Moby Dick,* the fiction of F. Scott Fitzgerald, and comments on Samuel Taylor

Coleridge, Samuel Johnson, and Edgar Allan Poe. A third part of the book is an excursion into pre-Columbian history in the mode of *The Sorrows of Priapus,* and the two essays in this vein seem quite out of place in this collection. *Alms for Oblivion* is essentially a rather loose compilation of Dahlberg's essays and has no central unifying theme. There is another perceptive introduction by Sir Herbert Read which points out the efficacy of the memoir as a vehicle of criticism. Read tells us that "because style is the man himself, a knowledge of the man is a key to his style." [5] Thus memoir and criticism are intimately related, and *Alms for Oblivion* illustrates such a relationship.

The first essay, entitled "My Friends Stieglitz, Anderson, and Dreiser," is a tender literary portrait of the "artistic life" of the 1920's and early 1930's. Dahlberg characterizes Waldo Frank, Ford Madox Ford, and Marsden Hartley (the American painter) as well as Stieglitz, Anderson, and Dreiser. His depiction here often centers around some physical trait which Dahlberg feels reveals a good deal about a man's character. Thus, we read much about Sherwood Anderson's "hot brown eyes," Hartley's "orgiastic nose," and Alfred Stieglitz's "doll-like wrists." A warm and somewhat nostalgic description of Dahlberg's friendship with Theodore Dreiser leads to a digression on the femininity of our literature, a theme developed at greater length in *Can These Bones Live.* All of the artists discussed in this essay are treated with respect, warmth, and admiration. Unlike the acerbic invective of *Truth Is More Sacred,* the prose of *Alms for Oblivion* is tempered with considerably more kindness.

Even those writers of whom Dahlberg is critical receive somewhat less severe treatment. His essay about William Carlos Williams, for example notes the lack of "moral force" in *Paterson* and in *The Later Poems;* but Dahlberg predictably speaks favorably of *In the American Grain.* While he is unenthusiastic about the remainder of Williams's work, he obviously feels a certain attachment to the man.

One of the most interesting essays in the collection is "No Love and No Thanks," which begins as an argument for the preservation of literary landmarks but quickly becomes a condemnation of the self-centeredness of our writers. Regarding the first point, Dahlberg remarks that "Students learn more reverence, homage, and courtesy from contemplating a house, a room, or a desk used by a Melville, a Whitman, a Poe, than from a congealed, academic reading of the *Iliad*, or 'Ligeia'" (29). He sees our destruction of important literary landmarks as indicative of our lack of respect for learning. We live in an era of "no love and no thanks," one which lacks feeling and respect for the nobler things of life. Our writers themselves have turned their back on art and prostituted their literary talents whenever possible. For Dahlberg, few sins are less forgivable than venality; and he cannot condone the legion of contemporary authors who have abandoned their friends and deserted their art for lucre.

The reader of *Alms for Oblivion* will be curious to learn more about Robert McAlmon, author of *Being Geniuses Together*, *A Hasty Bunch*, and *The Distinguished Air*. McAlmon was a close friend of Dahlberg's and associated with him in Paris in the early 1920's. Along with John Herrmann, he is referred to in the preface to *Bottom Dogs* as having "a passion for what was called the American scene." [6] He is depicted in Dahlberg's memoir as a tragic figure—an artist who longed for the success which so consistently eluded him. At the time of his death in the early 1950's, McAlmon was a forgotten man, but his work is now beginning to receive some attention. McAlmon's only "fault," according to Dahlberg, was his desire to make money from his books and to become famous. While Dahlberg is quite unwilling to forgive other authors for the same desires, his tenderness toward McAlmon overcomes his tendency to censure. Dahlberg concludes his memoir with a bitter prognosis that McAlmon will finally achieve the fame he so eagerly sought, now that he is dead.

The essay "The Expatriates" re-creates the literary milieu of the 1920's in Paris and provides us with some insight into Dahlberg's decision during those years to become a novelist. After submitting several stories to *This Quarter* magazine, Dahlberg was encouraged by its editor, Ethel Moorehead, to try to write a novel. As mentioned earlier, the first part of this early attempt was published in *This Quarter* as "The Beginnings and Continuations of Lorry Gilchrist," and was later revised and expanded to become Dahlberg's first novel, *Bottom Dogs*. Also in this essay are extended portraits of John Herrmann, Emmanuel Carnevali (author of *A Hurried Man*), and Hart Crane. Like McAlmon, Crane led a tragic life which ended in despair and finally suicide. Dahlberg was nonplussed by Crane's homosexuality, but he found him a warm and worthy human being, whose early death was a major loss for our literature.[7]

"For Sale" is an essay which once again takes up one of Dahlberg's favorite subjects of attack—the academic establishment. As in *Can These Bones Live,* he judges the professors in our universities to be perhaps the greatest enemies of literature. In one of his sharpest diatribes, he charges that "They are a malignant sodality of commercial litterateurs that govern ideas, reputations, renown, and whose index expurgatorious is dictated by bile and mammon"(62). Naming names and citing instances, he bitterly denounces those "criticasters" whom he feels have abandoned literature for commercial gain—among them Edmund Wilson, Horace Gregory, Lionel Trilling, Clifton Fadiman, and Philip Rahv. Commercialism, he suggests, is the most consistent danger confronting the artistic talent. Books and money should have nothing to do with each other; for, when they do, it is always the former which suffer. Dahlberg finds it shameful that so many writers have succumbed to the lure of lucre.

A few "gallant publishers" have, however, resisted the lure and placed the state of American letters ahead of their moneymaking propensities. He cites Ben Huebsch, Thomas Seltzer, the Boni brothers, Horace Liveright, the early Harcourts, and Pascal Covici as "cavalier gentlemen of taste with a civil regard for American letters"(64). But these are few indeed, and most publishing houses are concerned only with the salability and not with the quality of the work they publish. "Mention a volume of verse to a publisher now," Dahlberg cynically concludes, "and he regards it as a sinister intimation"(66).

Dahlberg puts aside memoir in the next five essays in *Alms for Oblivion,* to don the mantle of literary critic. His short essay on what he calls the "peopleless fiction" of F. Scott Fitzgerald is reminiscent in tone of Dahlberg's remarks about other contemporary writers in *Truth Is More Sacred.* Appalled by Fitzgerald's current reputation in the universities, Dahlberg finds his fiction tedious and dull and, most condemning of all, devoid of believable people. In addition, he judges Fitzgerald's style banal and trite, citing examples to buttress his opinion. He concludes that the academic critics have made Fizgerald into a legend in our time, but that legend has nothing to do with the actuality of Fitzgerald's writing. His final comments about the subject degenerate into a species of invective that is unfortunately all too characteristic of Dahlberg's later writing: "When everybody wants to paint or write, the arts are very bad. If Lionel Trilling really loved literature he would stop writing. When a critic admires so bad a writer as Fitzgerald, he is simply confessing that he himself cannot write. Dr. Ha'penny Knowledge [Dahlberg's epithet for university professors] is too ambitious: as Dr. Emil G. Conason says, what ails him is literacy, which is fast becoming a national malady" (72). Is it superfluous to suggest that this kind of a critical approach tells us very little about F. Scott Fitzgerald?

A short essay on Thomas Holly Chivers and Poe is a good deal kinder in tone and calls our attention to his biography of Poe, which Dahlberg feels has long been neglected. Lest this brief excursion into literary appreciation lead us to believe that Dahlberg is softening, he follows quickly with a sketch of William James entitled "Cutpurse Philosopher" which implicitly calls James' motives into question, suggests that he was a plagiarist, and asserts "that pragmatism is a credo for men with equivocal ends in mind"(78).

A remembrance of Randolph Bourne parallels Dahlberg's essay on Bourne in *Can These Bones Live*. Here he reiterates his earlier attack on the state and on the machinery of war. He speaks of the *Untimely Papers* and the *History of a Literary Radical* as books which speak to our time and deserve much more attention than they have received. Dahlberg also writes fondly of Mrs. Trollope's *Domestic Manners of the Americans,* a book which he obviously admires. Both the nineteenth-century English aristocrat and Dahlberg decry the same kind of shortcomings in America—the lack of culture and taste, the tendency to exalt the average which leads to mediocrity and monotony, and the lack of warmth and gratitude. Dahlberg's laconic conclusion is that Mrs. Trollope was correct about America, but she "only told those truths that have come from our own indigenous seers whom we have canonized, but not heeded"(90). We can garner similar facts about the American character from Twain, from Ambrose Bierce, from Stephen Crane; but somehow, Dahlberg suggests, we respond more readily to criticism from the outside.

Another bit of social criticism emerges from an essay on "Our Vanishing Cooperative Colonies" which laments the lack of community in modern American life—the separation of Americans from one another. Dahlberg reconstructs a brief history of our nineteenth-century utopian movements and sees them as reflecting a brief period in our culture during which men attempted to live together in harmony. This "gospel of being together which these people practiced is perhaps the most noble effort the American has made"(101). But the experiment was doomed to failure because America had already committed herself to the "progress" of the industrial revolution; and, with the coming of machines and industry, competition became the keynote of industrial progress and men could no longer live in communal togetherness. Quite in keeping with the thrust of Dahlberg's indictment of modernism, this historical essay accurately captures the meaning of our utopian experiments; and it inevitably makes us nostalgic about an age less preoccupied by the machinations which isolate man and make community impossible.

Two essays, "Florentine Codex" and "Beyond the Pillars of Hercules," which deal with pre-Columbian civilization in America, seem oddly out of place in this collection and would more comfortably fit in *The Sorrow of Priapus*. The former relates the importance of a little-known work about the Aztecs written by a sixteenth-century Franciscan monk. The latter relates the early history of Florida to "the lore of the Americas." Restating a point made many times in *The Sorrows of Priapus*, Dahlberg tells us that "The enigma of North American literature is to be comprehended by putting one's ear to the savage ground, for American writing is aboriginal rather than reflective or homiletical"(114).

Possibly the most controversial piece in this collection is a revaluation of Melville's masterpiece entitled "*Moby Dick:* A Hamitic Dream." Originally written for Stanley Burnshaw's collection, *Varieties of Literary Experience,* Dahlberg's criticism relies less on invective and more on careful literary analysis than do some of his other literary essays. Dahlberg's argument is forceful and convincing—so much so that Sir Herbert Read comments in the preface: "I confess I had always shared the common admiration for Melville's allegorical epic, but never was an illusion of mine so immediately shattered"(ix). Unlike his critical evaluation of Fitzgerald, Dahlberg's remarks are formidable because they come from a man who admires Melville's great achievement, although in the last analysis he judges *Moby Dick* to be an epic failure.

His charges are explicit and direct. *Moby Dick* is criticized for its lack of action and humor; for its inconsistent and ambiguous characterization; for its "shabby writing"; and, finally, for its sterility. Dahlberg finds the book the epitome of our "womanless literature." Each of these shortcomings is illustrated through specific examples from the novel. Regarding the lack of action, for example, Dahlberg comments, "Of the hundred and thirty-one chapters, only the last three before the Epilogue are about the pursuit of Moby-Dick, and the *Pequod* is always in the calms. . . . There is no motion in this novel, without which there cannot be any positive affection or heat in the mind"(118). Although the last part of this charge may be somewhat cryptic, it does seem surprising that a book which is supposedly the epitome of the adventurous chase novel is so devoid of action and motion. Few also would disagree with the second charge, that Melville's writing is often digressive and verbose, and often overly solemn. Dahlberg's critique of Melville's ambiguous characterizations seems less substantial. Certainly it is easy to counter that ambiguity was exactly Melville's intention, for he sees human nature in its complexity rather than in its simplicity and finds it impossible to reduce his characters to a series of uncontradictable attributes.

Finally, while it is easy to agree with Dahlberg's contention that *Moby Dick* is a "womanless book," I feel that he makes a bit too much of this. It is somewhat like lamenting the lack of femininity in the construction industry. As a book about whaling, *Moby Dick* is necessarily devoid of women. Dahlberg may be right when he asks "Who wants to chase a Sperm-Whale for over five hundred pages when he can pursue a Shulamite, a Cressid, a dowdy or a shake-bag?"(134); but if that is our intention then we should not be reading novels about whaling. In a word, though Dahlberg's critique of *Moby Dick* seems overly severe, it is not without point and relevance. Given wider circulation, it may well cause us to take a fresh look at Melville's art, unhampered by the biases with which recent criticism has surrounded it.

The final essay in the collection, "Allen Tate, The Forlorn Demon," is the only discussion of a contemporary literary figure in the collection. The essay deals with Tate's critical opinions rather than with his poetry and is strikingly more academic in tone than most of Dahlberg's essays. It is a gloss on Tate's opinions of Coleridge, Johnson, Poe, and other writers, with Dahlberg sometimes agreeing and sometimes taking issue. Clearly less substantive than the best essays in *Alms for Oblivion,* it concludes the collection rather anticlimactically.

*Alms for Oblivion* was published in the same year as *Because I Was Flesh,* and it has understandably been dwarfed by Dahlberg's achievement in the autobiography. As Frank MacShane points out, however, it is an extremely useful book "in defining Dahlberg's position as a writer." [8] The autobiographical essays particularly provide us with a logical counterpart to the events of Dahlberg's earlier life related in *Because I Was Flesh.* Like *Truth Is More Sacred,* the criticism is sometimes provocative and engaging, sometimes dense and beside the mark. It lacks the unity and stylistic brilliance of the autobiography, a work in which Dahlberg's style, subject matter, and theme complement one another to produce what is surely his masterpiece.

# CHAPTER 7

## *Bottom Dogs* Revisited

THE late Josephine Herbst tersely described the major difference between the novelistic treatment of Dahlberg's Kansas City boyhood in *Bottom Dogs* and the autobiographical treatment in *Because I Was Flesh:* "If the entire emphasis has shifted from the antipathies and revulsions of *Bottom Dogs* to the luminous insight of *Because I Was Flesh,* it is because Dahlberg himself had changed over, or, as the German expressionists would have it, had made a break-through." [1] What this change-over or "break-through" involves, it seems to me, is a synthesis of the best aspects of Dahlberg's writing. He had given us before a Realistic portrayal of his formative years in the three early novels, and he had made effective use of myth and legend in *Can These Bones Live* and *The Sorrows of Priapus;* but never before had he been able to bring the two together in such perfect balance and proportion. The attempted fusion of myth and reality which fails to affect us in *The Flea of Sodom* is here thoroughly successful because Dahlberg's style had matured in the intervening years and because the allusions in the autobiography have become an integral part of the subject matter.

There seems little disagreement that *Because I Was Flesh* is Dahlberg's masterpiece—the work which strikes us almost immediately as the culmination of all his writing and the one in which subject matter and style are uniquely wedded to create a vibrantly "real" portrait of his early life while, at the same time, infusing that portrait with mythological overtones growing out of a profoundly tragic vision of man's lot. Alfred Kazin has noted that Dahlberg's "own life is his most dependable text." [2] Indeed it is, and in writing of this life and its fabulistic dimensions he creates the work most likely to endure.

## I *Portrait of Lizzie*

In some ways, *Because I Was Flesh* is more biography than autobiography because it is primarily a book about Lizzie Dahlberg rather than about Edward. It is significant, I think, that Rodolfo Wilcock's Italian translation of the book is entitled *Mia madre Lizzie*. Dahlberg's mother emerges from these pages as a character with mythic dimensions, the embodiment of human suffering and endurance. Her will to live and her retention of hope for a better life stay with her in the face of strenuous odds and in conditions of intense loneliness. We have read her story before in *Bottom Dogs* and *From Flushing to Calvary*, so the events related are not new; but the manner in which they are presented infuses them with additional significance and gives them a much greater impact.

Paul Carroll has perceptively analyzed the additional levels of meaning in *Because I Was Flesh* as compared to the earlier works in an excellent introduction to *The Edward Dahlberg Reader*. Dahlberg describes Lizzie as "the three Marys of the New Testament," and Carroll takes this cue and extends the analogy as he sees it developing in the autobiography:

> To call one's mother the Three Marys of the New Testament is either to invite ridicule (which the author never encourages) or to insist on a dimension which could prove a disaster in the hands of a lesser writer. But as the events of Lizzie Dahlberg's life are told—how she abandons a doltish husband and two infants to run away with a dude barber, and how later, alone, she bears Edward in a Boston charity hospital; how she eventually settles in Kansas City, Missouri, where amid shabby respectability, greed, and vice, she labors as a lady barber and strives to raise her boy and to acquire a new husband; how rotten luck dogs her as suitor after suitor disappoints her, including the last one, a dotty, stinging, rich merchant named Tobias Emeritch, whose wooing of Lizzie provides one of the high moments of comedy and pathos in our literature; how she dies old and alone, in pain, half-crazed —as these events unfold Lizzie Dahlberg *becomes* the three Marys of the Gospels. She becomes Mary the Virgin Mother in that the author, like Jesus, feels that no man really possessed her but himself; Mary the Magdalene in that a stable of suitors actually copulated with her; and Mary the sister of Lazarus in that the author by conjuring back the ghost of his boyhood is her

brother, and during the hobo wanderings of his young manhood he is always dead, like Lazarus, until he returns home to her.[3]

Carroll's interpretation of the mythic dimensions of Lizzie Dahlberg is quite accurate, and few readers will not perceive a symbolic level in Dahlberg's portrayal of her. But the mastery of the portrayal is achieved because the reader comes away with a vivid impression of Lizzie as flesh and blood; it is her reality that remains with us, her physical presence which dominates many pages of the autobiography. She is surely no shadowy allegorical stereotype. Lizzie may be "the three Marys of the gospel," but she is first and last of all Lizzie Dahlberg; and the successful combination of these two aspects of characterization makes her unforgettable.

This dual aspect of Lizzie's portrayal is an excellent example of the balance between myth and reality that Dahlberg achieves throughout *Because I Was Flesh.* He is able to present both conceptions virtually simultaneously, one continuously complementing and enriching the other. The allusions in the autobiography are not pedantic exercises intended to reveal the author's erudition; they emerge as a natural expression of true feeling. Dahlberg's early descriptions of Kansas City, for example, are couched in mythical terms with comparisons made to Homer's Athens and ancient Palestine. The idea of making such comparisons may seem pretentious, but the reader quickly becomes convinced that Dahlberg truly sees the city in these terms, and the description does not assume the character of an affected literary pose.

In keeping with his "classical" reconstruction of Kansas City, is Dahlberg's view of the function of the autobiography. He regards it as enabling him to experience a catharsis to be rid of the "burden of Tyre in my soul." [4] The two most persistent themes of the work are introduced early: the depiction of Lizzie as a "luckless soul" and the author's search for self-identity. Perhaps because of his years in the Cleveland orphanage, and surely because of his meager knowledge of his father, much of Dahlberg's life has been a quest to answer the question "Who am I?" *Because I Was Flesh* is an attempt to provide an answer. He begins recalling his desperate plea to his mother while still a child, "Mother, have I no uncle, aunt, or cousin? Are you an orphan mother?"(5). Since Lizzie Dahlberg's identity and Dahlberg's own may be discovered in the meaning of their lives, the unraveling of past events presents some clue to the answer to this question.

The story of Lizzie's life in Kansas City is familiar from *Bottom Dogs,* and some of the same characters are introduced here—Max Stedna, the livery stable owner; Emma Moneysmith, a Mormon lady barber employed by Lizzie; and Harry Cohen (spelled "Coen" in *Bottom Dogs*), the owner of a "high class" bakery. Others reappear with different names, but essentially the milieu is the same one described in Dahlberg's initial novel. Here, however, he penetrates the essence of his material much more concisely and accurately. The events described in some 562 pages in the two early novels are here related in a good deal less than half the space, with very little omitted.

Chapter III, for example, which deals with Dahlberg's experiences at the Cleveland orphanage is a condensation of four chapters from *Bottom Dogs.* He re-creates the world of the Star Lady Barbershop with an economy of detail that he was not yet capable of in the apprentice work: "The circulation of money in the Star Lady Barbershop was sound though corrupt; currency was always in good health there because it was never stagnant. The lady barbers stole from Lizzie, and she took what she could from them—plus a bit of interest to which she felt she was entitled. One has to have indignation to steal with virtue"(29). There is no lengthy journalistic account of the actual stealing, and more of Lizzie Dahlberg's character is revealed in the final sentence than is suggested by pages of description in the earlier novel. In a word, what is omitted from *Because I Was Flesh* is the wealth of Naturalistic detail that characterized *Bottom Dogs.*

Dahlberg's bitterness toward his father because of his treatment of Lizzie is more apparent here than in the novels. Saul is described in the harshest of terms, and his physical description corroborates his personality. Dahlberg focuses on the animal-like qualities of his appearance—his shining teeth and beadlike eyes. He notes that the "faintest symptoms of rot" were beginning to appear in his face, and he emphasizes his instinctually animalistic behavior. "Saul," Dahlberg writes, "was some baleful seminal drop of a depraved rotting forefather; he lived solely to discharge his sperm" (44). Time and again he abandons Lizzie because he cannot resist chasing "chippies" all around the country. He returns only when he needs money, and then only momentarily. Saul *uses* Lizzie, and Dahlberg cannot forgive him for having done so.

Dahlberg's intense feeling for his mother manifests itself in many ways. The insistent fact of Lizzie's aging, so pervasive a theme in *From Flushing to Calvary,* becomes even larger in scope and relates ultimately to the title of the autobiography, taken from the Book of Psalms: "because I was flesh, and a breath that passeth away and cometh not again." From the very beginning, Dahlberg insists that Lizzie's experience, forlorn and woeful as it is, is an incontrovertible fact of human existence—a sadness which is the very stuff from which life is made. "Each one carries his own sack of woe on his back, and though he supplicate heaven to ease him, who hears him except his own sepulchre?"(2).

The interdependence between the mother and son also furnishes much of the book's drama. Lizzie looks to the young Edward for comfort and care. The son is ambivalent: he is attracted and repelled, loving and ashamed. Every time he looks at his mother's aging face and at her slovenly clothes, he is resentful and embarrassed. At the same time, however, there is a deeply rooted familial attachment within him. He is equally ashamed that he is unable to ease the pain or to offer his mother the security and assistance she so desperately needs. "O my God, and my heaven, there is my son," Lizzie ruminates, "if he could only come to my rescue"(195). The feelings of attraction and revulsion for his mother continue to vie with each other in the boy's mind: "My mother's appearance humiliated me"(154) and "When I considered my mother's privy sheets and illicit pillowcases I abhorred them . . ."(155). But a few sentences later the tenderness returns as Dahlberg is able to comment upon the situation from a distance and to relate the man's feelings rather than the boy's. Evaluating his youthful attitudes from this perspective, Dahlberg writes: "I refused to see that a grim angel had warped my mother's luck, and that she was deprived of one constant man who would cherish her paps."

His memories of Lizzie, however, are not all bleak and despairing. There are many episodes which are a good deal less somber, and several are frankly hilarious. The sketch of Lizzie's courtship with Tobias Emeritch is a sustained caricature, but one which is completely convincing. Dahlberg carefully builds on the humor of this timid and pathetic miser, whose eccentricities defy understanding. Afraid to make any major changes in his life, Tobias is confronted with the hard rationality of Lizzie, who is determined to snare a marriage agreement from him. They negotiate back and forth for a better bargaining position, Tobias dreading the thought of marriage, Lizzie anxious for security and companionship in her old age.

Finally, Lizzie confronts him with the idea of arriving at some written agreement: "Thoroughly impatient, Lizzie got a pen and a bottle of Waterman's ink: 'Can you make up your mind, mister? This is no romance, and it's not strictly business either; but what's right is right. It may be that you're too cautious and you will discover that nobody in the world will look out for you but me, and if wed, am I not entitled to something? We're a lost couple, worse apart than together. Be noble, please, and set aside a few stocks and shares, a few thousand dollars' "(194).

But, as Tobias "finds matrimony despicable from almost any point of view"(191) and lives by a credo that "One should postpone every decision in order not to make a mistake"(194), Lizzie is unsuccessful. The humor of the entire incident is finally undercut by the death of Tobias, several months after he has stopped calling on Lizzie. She reads about his death in the paper; and, if the autobiography can be said to have an epiphany, surely it is this moment: "Her face was immutable, and when her son turned away from the window, she took her hand from her throat which looked as though it were pieces of threadbare woollens she had patched together. She whispered, 'My son, I am an old woman' "(207).

## II *"I Am a Shade"*

I have been describing *Because I Was Flesh* thus far as a book about Lizzie Dahlberg; and, although she is clearly the dominant presence in the autobiography, by its very nature it is as well a portrait of Edward Dahlberg, of the events and discoveries which made a difference in his life. In this sense, the book follows the pattern of a "novel" of initiation in which the hero, in a search for self-identity, makes significant discoveries about the world around him. These discoveries grow out of the more meaningful experiences of an individual's life; and, for Edward Dahlberg, the first "event" to make a significant impact on his impressionable mind was his confinement at two orphanages, a Catholic asylum in

Kansas City, and, for a more extended period, the Jewish Orphan Asylum (J.O.A.) in Cleveland.

I have already suggested that this experience is described here in a more concise and condensed form than in *Bottom Dogs*, but in addition there is a degree of objectivity and separation from the material. In 1928, when Dahlberg wrote *Bottom Dogs*, the orphanage experience was perhaps still too close for him to arrive at any conclusions concerning its significance for his later life. Here he is able to intervene in the narrative from time to time to evaluate the events he is describing, to tell us the lessons he has learned from them. Thus, after a chapter describing the routine of life in the Jewish orphanage, Dahlberg interjects: "Our past is our only knowledge, and, good or ferocious, it is, for sublime or baleful purposes, the sole viaticum of the spirit. We can digest our childhood but never our present deeds, because no one knows what he is doing while he is doing it. The present is an absolute sphinx to men" (89–90). He concludes the chapter by emphasizing the continuing impact of the experience on his life: "He left the Jewish Orphan Asylum, but he was never to obliterate its hymn, because all experience is holy unto the heart which feels"(90).

It may be noticed that this sentence is written in the third-person point of view, and this is characteristic of the early part of the book. There is a distance between the author and the boy described in *Because I Was Flesh*, and Dahlberg stresses this difference by referring to himself as a boy in the third person for the first three chapters. The boy here is what contemporary psychologists would call Dahlberg's "inner child of the past," not the mature author of the autobiography. After he leaves the orphanage and enters "manhood," Dahlberg changes to first-person narration. The concept of an individual's relationship to his earlier life is at bottom a philosophical one, and the subject is explored here with probity and intensity.

In a Wordsworthian vein, Dahlberg writes: "Nobody ever overcomes the phantasms of his childhood. The man is the corrupt dream of the child, and since there is only decay, and no time, what we call days and evenings are the false angels of our existence. There is nothing except sleep and the moon between the boy and the man; dogs dream and bay the moon, who is the mother of the unconscious. . . . What is the space between the boy and the man? Did the child who is now the man ever live?"(49–50). The question of the relationship of the man to the boy that he is describing is central to the autobiography, but Dahlberg arrives at no conclusive solution to it. To what extent are our lives continuous, he asks; and how closely are we connected to our own pasts? "How many epochs are there in a man? . . . What remains of that boy who flits like a sapless phantom through my memory? I am more familiar with Theophrastus, Bartram or with Thoreau than I am with him"(122).

The transition from youth to maturity takes place at the beginning of Chapter IV in which the narrative moves from third- to first-person point of view. Dahlberg describes his return to Kansas City after six years at the orphanage—his first step in the realization of an identity. Throughout the orphanage years, he had been called simply "Number 92," and now he takes the name Edward Dahlberg: "After Ishmael, Number 92, was confirmed and had left the orphanage, he returned to Kansas City, his mother and Henry Smith, and went by the name of Edward Dahlberg. I had been nameless since birth and had only that knowledge of myself which I had derived from the streets, towns, stables and rivers I had known. I have avoided the use of 'I' because I was obscure to myself, and no Pythian oracle either then or now has helped me"(92).

Dahlberg describes his sexual awakening and early sexual experiences with considerable unease. He consistently "mythologizes" sex, almost as if to avoid speaking about it directly. In keeping with the theme of *The Sorrows of Priapus* are his lamentations about man's essential animality: "We are the sons of Adam, and when we long for a chine of beef, will Anaxagoras do? Seneca would make wise reading did not man scratch himself. Aristippus the Cynic said that the body is the *summum bonum* of man"(97). After a long description of his wanderings about the streets of Kansas City in search of a prostitute, Dahlberg becomes so self-conscious of his subject matter that he reminds his readers of his intentions: "Let nobody think I am peddling my impudicities for the few pennies a truthful author gets in this world"(100).

At the age of eighteen, Dahlberg left Kansas City and took to the road; and many chapters of *Bottom Dogs* are again, compressed into many fewer pages. He discusses the pain of separation from his mother, but he sees it as a necessary step toward self-fulfillment and independence: "I was fleeing from her to find my life"(115). The emptiness and frustration of life on the road is related with much the same feeling as in *Bottom Dogs,* but the added mythical dimension gives the experience a greater universality. Dahlberg compares America's midwestern towns to the seven divisions of hell in the *Talmud.* He speaks of his search for "the seven cities of Cibola"; but, like the early explorers of the New World, he finds his dream elusive and unattainable. His tortured cry—"Oh, where was I going?"—is the keynote of these vagrant, searching days of his youth and of his trek through these identical and heartless towns.

In 1919 he arrived in Los Angeles without money and tired of life on the road. Weary, broke, and yearning for inward peace and human companionship, he decided to stay for more than the customary week or so. At the YMCA he met his first "mentor," a sophisticated young man named Lao Tsu Ben. Ben seems to be the model for Max Maxwell in *Bottom Dogs,* but he is now depicted as much more cultured and intellectual. He introduces Dahlberg to the Classics and advises him to go to the university at Berkeley.

Dahlberg's experiences at Berkeley, hardly mentioned in the novels, are briefly described; and we discover the roots of his antiacademic feelings. Matriculating at the age of twenty-one, Dahlberg came to the academic scene slightly later than average and without the customary formal educational background. To this point, he had been largely self-educated; and he was unused to the rigors of an academic discipline. "What need had I," he writes, "of the sour pedants of humid syntax, or of courses in pedagogy, canonized illiteracy?"(143). Finding the courses at Berkeley "tiresome and bootless," and distracted by several inconsequential love affairs, he shortly left Berkeley to go to New York, where he obtained his bachelor's degree from Columbia in 1925.

Before arriving there, however, he stopped to visit with his mother in Kansas City; and his ambivalent feelings for her again come to the surface. The visit comes at a crucial and transitional time in Dahlberg's life, and it evidently made a significant impact on his memory. Indecisive about pursuing a college career, uncertain of his identity, and longing for purpose and meaning in life, he makes Lizzie the focus of his frustrations: "My life was a heavy affliction to me at this time; the chasm between my mother and me had widened. I blamed her for everything; whom else could I find fault with except my sole protector?" (163–64). He rails at Lizzie again and again because she did not provide him with a family—as if Lizzie's yearning for familial ties are any less than his own. There is a pervasive sadness about both the young man and his mother, who at this time have difficulty communicating because their worlds are moving further and further apart. There is pathos also in the young man's catalogue description of the living-room furniture as his only "relatives"—the table, his aunt; the cut-glass bowl, his sister; the settee, his cousin. "What an orphan I would have been," Dahlberg ironically comments, "without this familied room" (167).

Toward the end of Chapter IX, Dahlberg offers a concise statement of the essence of *Because I Was Flesh* which summarizes the intense quest for self-identity that epitomizes the autobiography. He has been pleading with Lizzie to reveal the true identity of his father; but, when Lizzie remains mute, he can only speculate about Saul the barber. He longs to be more certain because, in Dahlberg's credo, knowledge of parents is the first step to self-knowledge. But Lizzie refuses to respond.

> When I turned toward her, all my interred bones groaned: "I am a man, and there are ghosts of trees and a ravine howling within me, and at the root of a mountain sits a man. Who is he? You have always talked to me about your father, sisters and brothers, but I never saw one of them. What relations have I ever had or touched or smelled? In what city are my father's footprints? Does he walk, does he breathe, and is he suckled by the winds? See, I am a shade emptied of ancestors; I am twenty-three years old and grown into full sorrow." (168)

"I am a shade," Dahlberg laments, searching in vain for any clue to his origins.

The concluding chapter of the book is virtually the whole of *From Flushing to Calvary* condensed and rewritten. This chapter begins in 1926 with Dahlberg settling in New York with his mother near Calvary Cemetery in Queens. Lizzie's second husband, Popkin, returns for another try at their marriage; but both have become far different people than they were when they first married. Dahlberg briefly describes his own first marriage to a nameless woman in New York, and it is indicative of the degree to which his mother dominates the center of his mind that this woman is hardly mentioned; and, when she is, it is simply as "my wife."

Lizzie becomes ill and dies after Dahlberg relates a remarkable vision in which he sees Saul appear before him in the form of a fragmented worm: "When I bent over to caress the worm, it was piecemeal, and I turned my eyes against my breast and watched the various bits of myself crawling into the ground. Then I heard it say: 'I am Saul your father. Though I have sinned much, do not renounce me lest you mangle your own worms; no man can flee from his own worms and not be an evil to himself' "(217). In the dream, Dahlberg next sees Jesus of Nazareth, and he draws analogies between himself and Christ, their common suffering and fatherless lives.

The autobiography concludes with a moving tribute to Lizzie which may serve as her epitaph: "When the image of her comes up on a sudden—just as my bad demons do—and I see again her dyed henna hair, the eyes dwarfed by the electric lights in the Star Lady Barbershop, and the dear, broken wing of her mouth, and when I regard her wild tatters, I know that not even Solomon in his lilied raiment was so glorious as my mother in her rags *Selah*"(233–34).

## III *The Style*

In several of his letters, Dahlberg has been critical of the fact that American writers often write again and again the same book but in different guises. To Isabella Gardner he asserted that "The tragedy of American Literature is that no one writes more than one book." [5] And to Josephine Herbst he comments, "Our tragedy, really the American tragedy, is that we cannot seem to produce a writer who ripens." [6] Both of these ideas seem appropriate in discussing *Because I Was Flesh.* In terms of subject matter, it is indeed the "same" book that Dahlberg had written in the late 1920's and early 1930's; but, in terms of style, the author has indeed "ripened" and found a distinctive voice of his own. There are passages of remarkable similarity between *Bottom Dogs* and *Because I Was Flesh,* but the prose always is more "empassioned and elegant" in the autobiography.

I have already commented about the conciseness of the style here as compared to that of the earlier novels, but a comparison of two specific passages may illustrate the point more clearly. On first glance, it may appear that the material is expanded in *Because I Was Flesh* rather than condensed, but a closer scrutiny shows this is not the case:

| *Bottom Dogs* | *Because I Was Flesh* |
|---|---|
| When each fellow had made up his own bed, dressed, combed his hair and been inspected by the governor, they marched down double file to the basement playroom and shined their shoes. Each kid had a dauber and a brush. He spat on the black hair of the dauber which he dug into a community box of shoe polish; and if a guy was near-sighted, and stuck his nose down to the dauber to be sure he got the spit on the dauber and not on his shirt, Hans, if he was around, pushed the rest of his face into it. They smeared the polish and white plug of spit on the tops, sides, and heels of their shoes, and brushed them. (46) | After making up their beds and combing their hair, the orphans ran down to the basement. This was the playroom; there were long, rough wooden benches with boxes under the seat. Each box had a number—which became the boy's identity for his whole life in the orphanage. If the boy were talking or giggling, the governor or monitor cried out: "Number 92, quiet now, all in order!" In these boxes the orphans kept shoe polish—and marbles, ball bearings and stale Washington pies or doughnuts stolen from Becker's Bakery on Woodland Avenue. In the morning the boys would get out their daubers, spit on them and dig them into a tin of shoe polish. When a near sighted 5th grader, or a soft-witted half-orphan who wore glasses, spat on his own shirt or the pants of the boy next to him, someone would guffaw and a fight would start. (67) |

Dahlberg has apparently added many details to the passage from *Because I Was Flesh,* but they are details culled from many pages of the earlier novel. There are almost two pages in *Bottom Dogs* devoted to the theft of pastry from Becker's Bakery, but in the autobiography the matter is dismissed in a sentence. The only part of this passage which directly describes the situation as it occurs in *Bottom Dogs* are the last two sentences. The additions—

the standardized shoe boxes, the numerical identity of the boys—emphasize the monotony, anonymity, and inhumanity of life in the orphanage more effectively than entire chapters of *Bottom Dogs.* The bad grammar and the awkward syntax of the earlier passage are also replaced by smoothly flowing, articulate sentences which lack as well the repetition of harsh Naturalistic details.

Whatever observations we may make about these two passages, it is clear from the comparison that Dahlberg used *Bottom Dogs* as a source book for the autobiography. There are many other passages which could be placed side by side with similar results. Always there is less repetitive detail in the later work and less vernacular diction. The most striking difference in style, however, and one not illustrated by the passage quoted, is the natural use of myth and allusion. Nowhere in *Bottom Dogs* can we find prose like the following: "The playgrounds in back resembled Milton's sooty flag of Acheron. They extended to the brow of the stiff, cindered gully that bent sheer downwards toward a boggy Tophet overrun with humpback bushes and skinny, sour berries. Beyond the bushes was a pond close by a row of freight cars on a siding near the Standard Oil tanks. All this was as sacred to the children as Thoreau's Merrimac or Winnipiseogee rivers"(66). We might find the Standard Oil tanks and freight cars in *Bottom Dogs,* the flag of Acheron is likely to appear in *Can These Bones Live,* and the Winnipiseogee River would be at home on the pages of *The Sorrows of Priapus*; but it remained for *Because I Was Flesh* to bring them together in the same paragraph.

Allen Tate has commented on this quality of Dahlberg's style in his foreword to *Cinpango's Hinder Door.* After quoting a passage from *Because I Was Flesh* in which Dahlberg alludes to "the Cynocephali described by Hesiod and Pliny," Tate remarks: "The Cynocephali are not merely a learned and ornamental allusion, or vain indulgence of the vanity of the author. The Cynocephali are as real to Dahlberg as the wretched orphans. The lost moment in the orphan asylum is given a universal and timeless reality because it exists simultaneously with the dog-headed monsters of antiquity; it occupies the entire imaginative stretch between Hesiod and the Kansas City of the early years of this century." [7]

This "mythification of experience," as Alfred Kazin calls it,[8] transforms the particular experience to the universal. Dahlberg's suffering becomes the suffering of man; his despair, a lamentation over man's sorrowful fate. Because of this quality, the autobiography is not a Naturalistic tale of the Kansas City streets; nor is it a lofty allegory with little foundation in reality. In the fusion of the real and the mythic, Dahlberg has created in *Because I Was Flesh* his most important work—and a style that bears comparison to our most revered American literary classics.

## CHAPTER *8*

# Autobiography as Allegory

THE prefatory quote in *The Confessions of Edward Dahlberg* from Jacopo Sannazzaro's *Epilogue to Arcadia* reads like a familiar lament of modern poets about the loss of beauty, song, poetry, and the imagination in today's world. "Our Muses are perished," Sannazzaro writes, "withered are our laurels; ruined is our Parnassus: the woods are all become mute; the valleys and mountains for sorrow are grown deaf; Nymphs or Satyrs are found no more among the woods: the shepherds have lost their song." [1] Of course, Sannazzaro is not a modern but a Renaissance poet; and his conventional pastoral lamentation reminds us that poets have been bemoaning the state of our "botched civilization" for quite some time.

As a headnote to *The Confessions,* the quotation also suggests to the reader familiar with Dahlberg's earlier work that the book which follows will not be an autobiography that is larded with facts, statistics, places, names, literary gossip, and a reportorial account of events. Rather, as is the norm with Dahlberg, the prose will attempt to reawaken the deadened feelings within us by mingling myth, allegory, and elegance with the drab realities of a man's life. Arcadia may have vanished, but the artist's province is to find his inspiration in the universal verities of the human spirit; he need not concern himself with mundane trivialities.

*The Confessions* is divided into three sections: the first, by far the longest, is called "The Prentice Years"; the second, "Paris and London, From the Alone to Alone," is much shorter and focuses on Dahlberg's experiences in the late 1920's and early 1930's; the final section, "The Thirties, Penultimate Judgments," is the shortest, but it is the fullest account that we have of Dahlberg's participation in Socialist causes during the depression years. He has described these years in terms of his relationship to his mother in

*Because I Was Flesh.* Here his mother is rarely mentioned, and we become aware of other events in his life, especially of his associations with other writers. However, much of the material here has appeared elsewhere, especially in *Alms for Oblivion.*

As a sequel to *Because I Was Flesh,* I suspect there will be few readers to assert the superiority of the later volume, but *The Confessions* has its unique strengths, and, for generic innovation, it is Dahlberg's most audacious attempt. It is possibly the first time in English since John Bunyan's *Pilgrim's Progress* that a writer has made a serious attempt to link autobiography and allegory. This curious blend of genres has led one reviewer to comment that "The procedure piques, entices. At the same time it demonstrates the obvious: that allegory and autobiography can be mixed only to the detriment of both.[2] This view seems an extremely short-sighted one of Dahlberg's inventiveness; for the shortcomings of *The Confessions* do not grow out of the mixture of allegory and autobiography but from the fact that Dahlberg does not *sustain* the mixture throughout.

In the final chapter of the first section, Dahlberg abandons the allegorical motif and turns to a repetitious rehashing of the literary "gossip" that we are already familiar with from *Alms for Oblivion;* and there seems to me unquestionably a "falling off" from the imaginative dimension of the first section. In it, Dahlberg introduces himself as "Anybody's Miserable Chagrin," whose constant companion is "Alone" and who meets people like "Busy Perverse" and "Anonymous." In the last two sections, the personages are named—Charles Olsen, Edmund Wilson, Erskine Caldwell, and so on. What had been innovative, universal, imaginative, and audacious, becomes literary sniping—a catalogue of People Who Have Offended Me. In *The Confessions,* Dahlberg has really written two different sorts of books: one deals with his life as an emblem of human suffering; the other, with comparatively trivial grievances.

## I *"The Prentice Years"*

The opening chapter of *The Confessions* is a thematic overture to each of the book's sections. In it, Dahlberg asks the question that has occupied the attention of so many of our writers—it is as old as Homer, as modern as Bellow; and as we have seen, it has certainly been Dahlberg's principal concern: "Who am I?" However, here there is less search and an almost fatalistic acceptance of man's inability ever to answer that question. His opening paragraph, with its harrowing honesty, strikes his theme head on. It may also serve to remind us that the much discussed "identity crisis" of the 1970's has had a long history: "At nineteen I was a stranger to myself. At forty I asked: Who am I? At fifty I concluded I would never know"(3). Summarizing his youth as "a hemorrhage of melancholia" (what an evocative Dahlbergian phrase), he begins his "tale" in Los Angeles, when at the age of nineteen, he is seeking refuge from his world of loneliness, poverty, monotony, and despair. Readers of *Bottom Dogs* will notice the skeleton of Chapter XII of the novel beneath the events described here. The Los Angeles experience has also been related from a different perspective in Chapter VII of *Because I Was Flesh.*

As in *Because I Was Flesh,* a richly adorned prose is substituted for the journalistic jargon of the novel. Remnants of *The Sorrows of Priapus* and *The Carnal Myth* appear along the way, as in this pithy mixture of the aphoristic style and pre-Columbian history: "Regard the remnants of Tenochtitlan or a relic of Quetzalcoatl, and a man is merely contemplating his own ruins" (13). There is a good deal of the delightfully archaic diction we have come to recognize as a staple of Dahlberg's style, and there is a customary and characteristic lament at man's inability to surmount the longings of the flesh. But what gives *The Confessions* its distinction is Dahlberg's continuing talent for generic invention.

The linking of allegory and autobiography, which is certain to disturb some readers, surely separates and elevates the achievement here beyond Dahlberg's other work. He had used a similar technique unsuccessfully in *The Flea of Sodom* in which characters with heroic names struggle with the mundane reality of American life in the 1930's. *The Flea of Sodom* is essentially an allegorical fiction, a genre that writers like John Barth, Thomas Pynchon, Iris Murdoch, and John Updike have used and developed to a greater perfection than Dahlberg did. Here, however, the "characters" spring directly from the authors' recollection of his past; they are less imaginative constructs and more simply those essential qualities of an experience which remain with Dahlberg as he reconstructs it. He begins using this technique almost casually, causing the reader little adjustment: "My sole companions for months had been Hunger, who seldom left me without returning within the hour, and Meditation, who deserted me every day because, he complained, I had nothing to say he cared to recollect"(14). Thus far, this device is merely a vigorous and effective use of figurative language. By personifying the qualities he is writing about, Dahlberg makes them appear more vivid and real to the reader.

But two paragraphs later, the reader shares the narrator's astonishment as a character is introduced in fully allegorical fashion; and suddenly we seem to be thrust in the midst of a medieval morality play: "As Indigence is one of the most honest men I have ever met, I was stunned when he told me he was called Busy Perverse"(14). Initially, to be sure, this device requires some adjustment, for we are reading a book that presumes to be a "recollection of things past" and are confronted with an archaic literary convention, which may have served John Bunyan but which seems intrusive and anachronistic in the complex world of the twentieth century.

I was reminded of Dr. Johnson's well-known criticism of Milton's *Paradise Lost* in which he censures the author for mingling the allegorical personages of Sin and Death with the "real" character of Satan. Upon reflection, however, I have come to feel that the mingling of the "allegorical" and the "real" is a confusion not of Milton's but of Dr. Johnson's. In much the same way, the objection to Dahlberg's method here can come only from a literal-minded reader who refuses to acknowledge that a literary work is an autonomous effort of the creative spirit. The writer is free to create whatever worlds he wishes, mix whatever characters he chooses, describe any situation he feels will convey his vision. Satan, Sin, and Death are *all* characters in a literary work; each has an imaginative reality only. In much the same way, the "characters" in *The Confessions* are an imaginative rendering of the actualities of Dahlberg's past. Autobiography is a genre that we have generally relegated to a quasi-literary status. It is supposedly closer in kind to journalism than it is to fiction, poetry, or drama. But Dahlberg has clearly demonstrated in the first part of *The Confessions* (and, of course, in *Because I Was Flesh*) that it can be, at its best, a genre which draws upon as many of the artists' resources as any other. Again, we can recall the quotation from Sannazzaro and remember that the imaginative quality raises humdrum events to universal application. Dahlberg here wishes to bring back the "muses" which have departed.

The meeting with Busy Perverse represents Dahlberg's contact with the workaday world in America and his severe disdain for it. Perverse calls Anybody's Miserable Chagrin (read Dahlberg as artist) a "masterpiece of senility" and useless in terms of social need. Unlike the artist, Perverse has no vision, no solitude, no insatiable needs apart from his constant "busy-ness." Yet he is human, another living being, and can the artist reject humanity? It is a paradox which Dahlberg states succinctly: "Without question I detested him. But how could I satisfy my hunger for people" (21). The most reasonable response, I suppose, would be to find other artists; and, indeed, that is where Dahlberg does turn for friendship; but, with few exceptions, his human relationships have been luckless and short-lived. This antipathy between the artist and the world in which he lives is the theme of the early chapters of *The Confessions.* Summing it up precisely, Dahlberg writes, "When Busy Perverse informed me I did not understand the world, I asked him which one, his or mine. Did I not carry the universe within myself?" (23).

Finding it impossible to function in the busy-ness and perversity of American society, Dahlberg has turned increasingly inward and toward books for his solace; yet he pines for human companionship, and the desires of Priapus burn always. Torn between introspection and extraversion, Dahlberg's portrait of the artist as a young man is a familiar one; but the allegorical manner here gives it point and uniqueness.

Other allegorical personages that Anybody's Miserable Chagrin encounters during his "prentice years" are Anonymous, Alone (his constant companion), Humility, Compassion, Reason, Cash, Good Luck, Greed, and Optimism. In addition, there are many characters and events modeled after specific people and episodes from Dahlberg's life which are given an allegorical label that immediately conveys his attitude toward them. Thus Berkeley is Rabble University; Columbia, St. Pragma. The Berkeley and Columbia experiences are briefly described in Chapter VIII of *Be-*

*cause I Was Flesh,* but in none of the detail we find here. At Berkeley, Dahlberg, never missing an opportunity to attack academic pedantry, encounters Professor Smallhead, Pedagogue George Fundament, Dr. Burden Greybones, and Dean Percival Unconscious, among others; Columbia offers Dr. However Pointless, and Anathon All, "the eminent scholar of the doctrine of the Logos" (160).

The account of his university experience, along with two other episodes from Dahlberg's young manhood, constitute most of the "Prentice Years" section. The first of these is his initial sexual encounter with a lonely twenty-year-old in her apartment on Figueroa Street in Los Angeles. Again, *Bottom Dogs* is the source book; for the incident is a retelling of the "Solomon's Dancepalace" chapter of that novel. It is the note upon which the novel ends—Lorry's sexual desires frustrated as he wanders on Tenth Street in Los Angeles waiting for something to happen. In both books, the "affair" is not consummated because of Lorry's (Dahlberg's) inexperience and shame. Here, however, the episode is described with a tenderness and pathos that reflects the author's increased distance from the event.

Meeting the young lady in a sleazy Los Angeles nightclub, Dahlberg conveys the immediate sense of kinship he felt upon encountering another lost soul: "In a fret I happened to turn and saw a maid about twenty years old. Modestly I looked at her; now I was beset by Compassion, who hardly ever visits anybody. She, too, was a gull of nature and I guessed that no one looked after her but Alone. I thought I saw a wizened smile creep around the corners of her mouth" (49). They shortly leave for the girl's apartment, but a sexual relationship is impossible because the young man is ashamed of his lust, his mind on "higher things," his libido calling him to more insistent matters.

This division in Dahlberg's sensibility has received its most distinctive expression in *The Sorrows of Priapus*: "The human race has declining powers, and man resembles less the brute the more he approaches what we define as mind. He is an intermediate form; the highest man will have no scrotum; it is ludicrous for a moral philosopher to scrape and scratch as any worm" (52–53). The addition of humor in *The Confessions* also distinguishes the incident from the description in *Bottom Dogs.*

Much of the humor grows out of the lofty diction which accompanies the young Dahlberg's sexual advances and underlines the flesh-spirit dilemma which is confronting him: "I prize your celestial documents, your hips and potable nipples. Without lawless passions I swear by the discretion of your feet and your continent legs I adore you. Guileful as I am I shall never forget the forgiveness in your loins. I admit I become excited when I consider the rakish flea that perches inside your blouse" (52).

Despite the humor and the pathos, however, the incident conveys in some ways an even deeper sense of despair than the final pages of *Bottom Dogs*. At the conclusion of the episode, Dahlberg tries to befriend two vagrants who flee from him; this concluding vignette seems to emphasize the isolation of his spirit and his awareness of the difficulty he continually experiences about bestowing trust in people. Abandoned by both men and women, he is the archetypal alienated artist.

The second notable episode in the first section is another amorous encounter—this time with a young woman named Mary, the daughter of a tailor. Dahlberg's long conversation with the girl's querulous and distrusting father is one of the funniest episodes in the book, but it is also another instance of the conflict between the natural artist and a functionally ordered society that is indicative of the lack of communion and communication between the two. Yet this tailor is a remarkable and admirable man, whose primary concern is to see his daughter well married. He cannot help being confused by Dahlberg's evident lack of ambition in conventional terms. "Since I met you," he tells the young man, "I'm all mixed up. Are you trying to persuade me that to be poor is God's gift? Intelligent as you are, why are you stupid? Can't you do anything at all with yourself?" (91).

The father simply wants to know what the young artist can *do* for his daughter, and he cannot understand Dahlberg's acceptance of a state of perpetual poverty or his "uselessness" in terms of social utility. When he urges his daughter to abandon this ne'er-do-well, she listens to her father's advice. The humor quickly dissolves as we focus on one of the most sorrowful images in *The Confessions*—the description of the dejected and rejected young Edward, pitifully longing for a glimpse of Mary outside the place where she works:

> Stoical for four to five days, I then commenced to haunt the office of Western Union. She had left. I waited for hours outside that merciless slab, the door to the cottage. She never appeared.
>
> A dry-goods storekeeper pitying my plight said her parents had sent her to one of the canyons.
>
> In the evening I sat on the curbstone, my cankerwormed head in my arms. The Mojave Desert always would be within me. . . . (100)

The incident which began with images of vitality and passion ("I devoured her milked calves and was set afire by the rump Venus had given her to placate the hungry tribe of males. Filled with untasted myrrh I yearned to gather her mouth unto me" [75]), ends with a desert image of death and desolation. It is a paradigm for the failure of human relationships which has characterized Dahlberg's life from his early youth. In the end, the artist lives only with himself.

A third "self-contained" episode from the "Prentice Years" section is one I have already mentioned—the narrative dealing with Dahlberg's "venture upon the pikes of American education" (116), first at Berkeley, then at Columbia. Again he stresses his apartness from other people: "I lived entirely by myself, in a womanless world desolate as the northern regions of Hudson Bay . . ." (137). There are however, accounts of two relationships Dahlberg had with women during these years. The first he describes as "a virgin relationship" with Kate Carla. She is described with great tenderness, and the fond memories of their walks together are evidently a joy for Dahlberg to recollect. The second "affair" is a more sensual, though still unconsummated one, with a woman simply referred to as "G." Also in the college section are accounts of various professors that influenced Dahlberg at Berkeley and Columbia, and there is a rather extraordinary chapter on the decline of language (Chapter XVIII) which is not related to anything else in the book; but it sings out with Classical elegance Dahlberg's familiar credo—the decline of language is symptomatic of the decline of man.

The final chapter in the "Prentice Years" is also set apart from the others, and one reviewer has called it the book's "wittiest episode." [3] It involves Dahlberg's interaction with the world of commerce, and it describes in what may be a conscious self-parody his experiences trying to open up a bank account with twenty-five dollars. The opening paragraph with its circuitous pomposity contrasts the manner and the matter of the chapter nicely. Since there is no need to deal with mundane matters mundanely, Dahlberg—instead of telling us that "One Friday, I decided to open a bank account with my spare twenty-five dollars"—writes: "On a piscatorial Friday, when there was a mild consoling breeze blowing from the gray ruffled Hudson, and a rising of the Crab, I felt it was propitious to make a decision. With twenty-five dollars moldering in my pocket I entered the house of the moneychangers" (177).

The chapter, humorous though it is, is actually a serious comment on the degree to which modern man has substituted economics for religion. The bank is called "The Lord's Security Savings Bank," and the vice-president informs the potential depositor that "money is St. Paul's Epistle to the Romans" (178). The venality of modern man, which has been a frequent theme in Dahlberg's work, receives perhaps its most concise expression in the essay on "A Decline of Souls" in *The Leafless American.* This chapter in *The Confessions* is the culmination of that theme, and it is a fitting conclusion to his apprentice years as he deserts the world of lucre and commerce for the life of the artist. In it, he has underscored his agreement with the quotation from Baudelaire's *Intimate Journals* which serve as a headnote: "Commerce is Satanic, because it is the basest and vilest form of egoism" (177).

## II *The Naming of Names*

The allegorical method of *The Confessions* is dropped entirely in the second section of the book, which recalls Dahlberg's life abroad in the 1920's with other expatriates. The reader of *Alms for Oblivion* will recall many of the incidents related here from the chapter entitled "The Expatriates" in that work. In both places, Dahlberg recounts his relationships with Ethel Moorehead, Ernest Walsh, Emanuel Carnevali, Robert McAlmon, Hart Crane, and some others. The details are similar in both; and, unlike the material Dahlberg has reworked from *Bottom Dogs* and *From Flushing to Calvary,* there seems little stylistic change between the earlier version of these events and the manner in which they are described here. I cannot help but wonder why they are repeated here. There are, to be sure, some additional episodes described, and the reader does learn of several incidents which left an indelible impression of Dahlberg's psyche.

For example, it almost is painful to read his description of how he was crushed by William Carlos Williams's off-handed remark as Dahlberg was about to give a public reading from his novels and *Can These Bones Live*: "I was seated next to Williams and I began searching crazily for something in my books to read, perhaps a page or less if need be, for I was extremely nervous and did not want to bore my auditors or myself. I could not find anything I did not abhor. Williams, who could be enchanting or flinty, glared at me and hissed fiercely: 'For Christ's sake, are you going to read all three novels?'" (202). The simple fact that Dahlberg remembers this small incident, well over thirty years after the event, indicates how deeply he was bruised by what appears to be hardly a serious remark.

In the other new material in this section, Dahlberg describes his marital life. This is the first time he has done so in anything more than a cursory way. Although he deals with the subject very indirectly, Chapter XXVI is an account of the breakup of his first marriage with a woman who is unnamed and who is described only as "the near kin of a Cleveland industrialist." Chapter XXVII is also the first lengthy account of the way D. H. Lawrence came to write the preface to *Bottom Dogs,* and we learn in fact that it may have been Lawrence who gave the title to that novel. But, although Dahlberg does acknowledge Lawrence's genius in *Studies in Classic American Literature,* his attitude toward Lawrence is ambivalent, and he regards the preface to *Bottom Dogs* as a "long, hectic and cerebrated invective."

A final nugget in the section is a brilliant chapter, again not connected to anything around it, in which Dahlberg assumes an incantory style and chants a harrowing refrain "That's how it is with me," as he summarizes the woes of his life:

> My youth is clean gone, and for a cock of prose thin and dwarfed as the lichen in the Barren Grounds. I sigh for vision, and know not what shirt I wore that day. I examine my hands and wonder whose they are; my nose is a stranger to my face. When I think I know I do not know. If I am quiet, impatience were better; if choleric, it is a caggy day. That's how it is with me.

> I've got no theories to peddle, for I hawk parables, or chew my moldy weather, and that's good, too. That's how it is with me. (229)

This chapter ends the second section with the sense of a lost and woe-begotten time and with a kind of humility that should answer those of Dahlberg's critics who accuse him of arrogance. An extremely moving passage, it raises the second part of the book beyond the level of repetitiveness.

## III *The 1930's Once More*

Several times Dahlberg has written that American writers essentially write the same book again and again under different guises, but nowhere has he illustrated his perception so completely as in the final section of *The Confessions,* "The Thirties: Penultimate Judgements." Any reader of his earlier work cannot help being disappointed that he has chosen to once again go over situations and personalities he has described elsewhere (often in nearly the same words) and again stops relating the story of his life just before his most creative period begins. When are we to have Dahlberg's account of the 1940's and 1950's?—the years of his life that remain, apart from scant biographical details here and there, uncharted.

There are a few new items in these chapters. We learn of the MacDowell "plantation for authors" in New Hampshire where Dahlberg spent some time in 1930 in the cottage next to that of Edwin Arlington Robinson finishing work on *From Flushing to Calvary.* There is also an interesting account of his involvement in the famous (or infamous) *Scottsboro* case and a brief recollection of his living a short time (in 1933) in Paint Creek, West Virginia, a desperate, poverty-stricken mining town where he received the terrible news of Hart Crane's death from Malcolm Cowley.

Apart from these few events, however, almost everything in this section has been described or discussed elsewhere in Dahlberg's work. We read another attack on Edmund Wilson, James T. Farrell, and Erskine Caldwell—venal scribblers all, who deserted literature and offended Dahlberg in one way or another. Most vehement is the lengthy disparagement of Wilson, who has before been the object of Dahlberg's wrath in *Alms For Oblivion* and elsewhere. Again the attack is *ad hominem*: "The thought comes to me that American Literature might be different had Edmund Wilson had carnal lips" (245). I find it difficult to understand the cause of Dahlberg's bitter hatred of Wilson, although he tells us that these ill-feelings began when Wilson told him he had praised *Bottom Dogs* merely to sell books. Perhaps, but a nearly forty-year hostility based on what seems to be a momentary lapse of judgment hardly seems credible.

Dahlberg is equally caustic in his appraisal of the late Charles Olsen, whom he feels betrayed their friendship when Olsen received a modicum of literary fame. And again he points out the harmful influence of Communist and Marxist dogma on the arts, a subject he has dealt with at length many times before but most eloquently in the section entitled "Proletarian Eucharist" in *Can These Bones Live.*

The book concludes where it began, with a resigned self-acceptance, and with the fatalistic realization that human identity is as illusive as the wind, as impossible to define as the stars. There is a final and devastating dismissal of the impotence of human reason—its inability to provide us with the answers to any of the inexplicable mysteries of existence. It is the heart alone which teaches, which guides us through the most troubled of our days and enables us to endure.

CHAPTER 9

# A Miscellany

THE remainder of Dahlberg's work after *Because I Was Flesh* —apart from *The Confessions*—was published in various periodicals and is quite diverse. His aphorisms, collected in *Reasons of the Heart* appeared in *Arena, Kenyon Review, Dublin,* and other periodicals. His poetry, a selection of which was published as *Cinpango's Hinder Door,* has appeared in *Poetry, Antioch Review, Texas Quarterly,* and the *Massachusetts Review. The Leafless American* is a compilation edited by Harold Billings of essays, poetry, and reviews written for the most part during the 1950's and including some previously unpublished material. Dahlberg's letters, *Epitaphs of Our Times,* to which I have alluded throughout, were published by George Braziller in 1967. Thus, none of these later books is a unified, completely conceived whole. They are of interest to the student of Dahlberg's writing, however, because they illustrate his experimentation in various genres and serve as additional generic outlets for his major thematic concerns.

## I Reasons of the Heart

A book of aphorisms is almost impossible to discuss in a critical fashion—one either likes a proverb or he does not, either frames it above his desk or crumples it for the wastebasket. Dahlberg provides such a large variety for us to choose from that almost everyone will find some in this collection that will appeal to him.

*Reasons of the Heart* is divided into twenty sections, each containing aphorisms which deal with specific subjects. There are sections "On Writers and Writing," "On Sloth," "On Myth and Religion," "On Lust," "On Suffering," and so on. We immediately recognize that Dahlberg's favorite subjects are given suitable space. It is apparent also that the aphorism is not a new mode of writing for Dahlberg, as many of these sentences appear in only slightly altered form in other works. Anyone who has read *The Sorrows of Priapus, Can These Bones Live,* or *Because I Was Flesh* is certain to feel that he has heard many of these aphorisms before.

Frank MacShane has suggested that the aphoristic mode of *Reasons of the Heart* derives from Dahlberg's "conviction that America desperately needs a sense of direction and order." [1] He cites Dahlberg's remarks to the effect that America is a vast, chaotic continent, filled with a nomadic people. Contemporary life particularly is complex, various, and disordered; what is needed most is simplicity. The proverb or aphorism is the literature of simplicity. It enables the writer to cut through the complex and contradictory maze of a shifting reality to arrive at a glimmering truth which is so essentially true that it withstands the flux and transitions of various time periods.

It is easy to understand why the genre has not been overly popular in the twentieth century. In the eighteenth century and before, when man was a bit more secure about his position in the universe and about the very existence of "essential" or fundamental truths, the genre flourished. The tradition, a vital one from Marcus Aurelius to Ben Franklin, seems anachronistic in our own time because it is the genre of an age convinced that absolutes exist and that order is the defining factor of the universe. That Dahlberg attempts the genre in today's world may be anachronistic, but it corroborates his lament in one of the poems in *Cinpango's Hinder Door*: "By my soul I cannot endure the world, for I am absolute and not/relative." [2]

The section "On Writers and Writing" which begins the volume (and there is no indication whether these divisions are Dahlberg's or an editor's) contains some viewpoints which we find familiar. Sometimes these achieve eloquence: "Literature is the tragic sport of dust," [3] and sometimes they fail badly: "A painter can hang his pictures, but a writer can only hang himself" (9). Others are neither eloquent nor platitudinous but simply accurate: "Art must seem reasonable though man is not" (11). Dahlberg "On Love and Friendship" reveals a deeply rooted bitterness: "If you are looking for an enemy be kind, gentle and above all truthful" (21). His proverbs "On Lust" are entirely predictable for the reader of *The Sorrows of Priapus*: "What man's head would do is always defeated by his scrotum" (23).

Some of the aphorisms in the section "On Men, Women and Marriage" contain penetrating insights into human nature, but they reveal at the same time Dahlberg's rarely displayed sense of humor. This humor is particularly evident when he develops an idea at greater length than a sentence: "A husband may find his wife in bed with another and she will swear to the miserable cuckold that she and the man had taken ill and were forced to lie down or succumb to nausea or the most brutal headache. After listening to such outrageous protestations, the wittol is not absolutely certain that his wife has been false, and so they go on together—she committing adultery and he resorting to logic to prove to himself that she is faithful" (34). There is also advice for would-be adulterers: "The easiest way to seduce another man's wife is to praise her husband after which she will find your character very attractive" (36).

These few examples may suggest that the genre is more effective when it is taken rather lightly. There are many humorous moments in *Reasons of the Heart*, perhaps more than in any of Dahlberg's books; but there is also a good deal of weighty solemnity which gives the work a ponderous quality that makes it difficult to appreciate in toto. Dahlberg is effective and humorous when he tells us that "No female can tolerate a lover who after warming her with many caresses suddenly decides to protect her virtue" (37), or when he notes that "The supreme happiness of the ordinary man is an easy bowel movement" (74). But too often he sacrifices this levity and becomes overly didactic and cynical: "It is absolute folly to expect a good experience from a person with whom one has had a bad one" (61), or "Don't speak to me of kind and gentle nature. I only believe in an evil energy that is a man-eating Demiurge" (134).

It would be easy to continue citing examples from *Reasons of the Heart* to illustrate this or that point, but the reader would be better advised to peruse the volume itself. Some may find immortal words in it, others may consider it an anachronism, and still others may be openly antagonistic to its authoritarian tone. I find myself returning to it again and again because of the concise statements of Dahlberg's positions on various matters and particularly because of the accuracy of his comments on human nature. In a sense, however, the work is a regression, coming as it does after *Because I Was Flesh*. One of the primary reasons for the success of the autobiography is, as Josephine Herbst has pointed out, that "Dahlberg has taken the deadweight out of his teaching as a didactic writer, and has launched his basic theme on the confusing, chipping, and changing current of individual human life." [4] The didacticism happily absent in *Because I Was Flesh* makes an occasionally unwelcome reappearance in *Reasons of the Heart.*

## II Cinpango's Hinder Door

Dahlberg's only book of poetry is more structured than his collection of aphorisms, but the two volumes have much in common. The poetry in *Cinpango's Hinder Door* is epigrammatic and proverbial; and, like the aphorisms, it is calculated to instruct rather than to entertain. There are two types of poetry in the collection—long, allusive, erudite poems on pre-Columbian history and myth, and shorter personal lyrics which express Dahlberg's intense suffering, his feelings toward his mother and father, and his essentially tragic view of life. It is easy to agree with Frank MacShane who suggests that "the short lyrics . . . are those to which the reader is most likely to return. Free of what in some of the longer poems seems learning heavily worn, these lyrics have an emotional intensity that derives from actual experience." [5] These shorter poems are yet additional evidence that Dahlberg writes best when he writes about his own experience and puts aside the literary pose that characterizes *The Flea of Sodom* and some of the other writing.

In his short foreword to the poems, Allen Tate remarks that the myth of Cain and Abel is the central image which thematically links the poems with one another. Cain is a symbol of the present which has destroyed its connection with the historical past, which is symbolized by Abel. The past can be revivified only through myth and legend, and the function of literature is to attempt this revivification. Several times in the poems, Dahlberg makes explicit reference to the Cain story in terms that corroborate Tate's symbolic interpretation:

Who has been the Cain of stars?
Who slew the ground and sealed the springs
Where reedy, bellied nereids
Gave their teats to bud
In the hands of fisher-lads and lickerish Pan? (38–39)

And:

> O, the Cains,
> What have they done to the earth?
> Do I not hear the mangled tilth,
> The seed and the furrow piteously crying
> Like the lamb torn by the fox? (41)

And, in a poem on Walt Whitman:

> Every aged man was father Adam;
> He went soft upon the ground
> Lest he trample Abel's blood.
> ..........................................................................................
> We cannot bear each other,
> For we are immense territory,
> And our malignant folly was to mew us up in cities,
> And take away our ocean past.
> For the sign of Cain is solitude,
> And he that goes in the earth apart
> Grieves as the worm. (45–46)

Although there are other examples, these few may suggest the multidimensional quality of Dahlberg's use of this myth in the poetry. For, while Tate's reading is certainly correct, the myth also serves to symbolize man's inability to live in harmony, his inclination to violence, and his lack of familial ties. Each of these motifs is recalled again and again in the poetry, and the Cain story serves as a focal point for these interrelated themes.

In the first line of the title poem Dahlberg immediately establishes his connection to an American poetic tradition. He writes in Whitmanesque fashion,

> I chant energy and chance to youth,
> And to the old I bring
> The mulled wine of ancient annals. (15)

The poem is a reiteration of one of Dahlberg's most persistent themes—the need for man to find his identity through the rediscovery of a mythological past:

Sons of little-born dust,
Your birth is in the bones of gods and fathers
Whose annals you know not . . . (15)

Also Whitmanesque is the interspersion of prose passages which alternate with more formally structured stanzas. The intervening paragraphs are stylistically and thematically reminiscent of *The Sorrows of Priapus*; and, throughout the first part of *Cinpango's Hinder Door,* Dahlberg seems to be relying heavily on the earlier book. We suspect that many of these poems may have been written at approximately the same time as *The Sorrows.* Part two of the first long prose-poem in the collection sometimes reads like a textbook on pre-Columbian history, including the textbook techinque of setting off newly introduced words in italics. There are long catalogues of Aztec and Mayan names which give the poetry an exotic sound, but occasionally they render it difficult and pedantic: "Don Fernando entered the lagoon of *Dos Bocas* and founded *Mérida. Campeche, Cozumel, Champotón,* and the Sierra opposite *Mayapán* contained oratories that kindled Christian rages. At *Campeche* a temple stood in the sea and on its top steps sat an idol whose flanks two animals were devouring. The pyramids of *Chichén Itzá* and *Mayapán* were a seasoned art to match a Memphis or an Elephantine, and were groves for Baalim in the valley of Hinnom" (23). Edmund White's comments on another of Dahlberg's esoteric paragraphs may also serve here: "Upon confronting such a passage, the reader's first stunned reaction is to murmur, 'Come again?' " [6]

"February Ground" is a poem which attempts to reconstruct the symbolic genesis of the North American continent. Dahlberg's mentors are Hesiod and Strabo, and the poem is a geographic catalogue and a survey of natural history in North America. The title emphasizes what Dahlberg feels is the characteristic quality of the continent—its coldness, barrenness, and sterility. "North America," he writes, "is the February hemisphere

With rivers and skies of great water claws,
And bluffs that are steep rapids.
The woods lie close to the soul,
And only the moon to light its lakes
And oppose its shaggy head-winds.

There is no roadstead,
No passage out
Save beyond the furied bar outside Caudebac. (25–26)

The next poem, "Trust Is a Fool," takes a different direction. It is a series of what might be termed "personal aphorisms" which relate to or reveal particular aspects of Dahlberg's character. There are five long stanzas written in a Whitman-style free verse with little or no apparent connection between them. The "I" of the poem, however, does seem to take on a universal quality as a poem progresses, much like Whitman's "I" in *Song of Myself*. Dahlberg's "I," unlike Whitman's, laments rather than celebrates man's lot. In place of the cosmic optimism of Whitman's poem, what emerges from "Trust Is a Fool" is a deep sense of guilt and bitterness:

Whatever has happened in the world that is wicked or furtive or cozening, I have done it.
I am Barabbas whom the world regarded for more use than Jesus. I am Peter who thrice betrayed the son of God. (30)

A common theme of the four shorter poems which follow is the death of human affection. Again there is the personal lament, "I shed tears on the Mount of Olives because people no/longer care for each other . . ." (32). But there is a paradox in the attitude developed here as there is in much of Dahlberg's writing about human affection; for, although he longs for companionship, trust, and human warmth, Dahlberg himself admittedly finds it difficult to sustain any lasting personal relationships. He tells us that a mutual trust is the essence of friendship, yet he is reluctant to trust anyone. The paradox is best summed up in the fourth of these short poems in which he writes, "God forgive me for my pride; though I would relinquish my/own birthright for that wretched pottage of lentils which is/friendship, I mistrust every mortal" (34).

"Sing in the Beginning" returns to the theme of man's need to discover his origins. "These iron centaurs," he exclaims, speaking of modern man, "have lost their beginnings" (35). The poem becomes an extended attack on modernity, but it concludes on a very personal note. The final stanza contains a very moving description of a man past the prime of his life, moving inevitably toward old age, longing for whatever immortality his art can bestow:

> My elbows bend, aged in the rot of space,
> But I am not dead, being too small born,
> For dying is journeying to shoreless ends.
> There is sundown in my loins;
> The horse has ceased neighing in my thighs.
> I walk over desert cockle and tread the gourd,
> Seeking the cuneiform footprints
> Of prophets and maize kings.
> I am choked without the good savour of sages. (39)

These lines are additional evidence that Dahlberg's writing is most effective when it grows out of personal experience and attempts to capture the intensity of his feelings.

Two companion poems, "No Eye of Erebus" and "No Image in Sheol" again bewail man's lack of connection with place or with the past. In these poems, the "I," universal rather than personal, represents modern man who is "placeless, / Without kinly rock or pasture" (41). "No Image in Sheol," a poem biblical in tone and allegorical in method, is one of the most difficult in the collection. Dahlberg develops the idea that man's lust has destroyed his "remembering faculty" and has sowed confusion in the world. As his greed became insatiable, man became more dependent upon inventions and built cities, "The kilns, the pestles, the tools, Erech, Babel, and Ur" (44); and these destroyed his soul. The message is rather opaquely stated in symbols that strike one as forced and unnatural. A mountain, for example, is symbolic of lust; and the invention of language is seen as the father of all the world's ills.

Dahlberg's poem on Walt Whitman makes quite clear the indebtedness to the Whitman tradition that I have already mentioned. However, it should be evident from the poems already discussed and from Dahlberg's comments on Whitman in *Can These Bones Live* that he does not embrace Whitman wholeheartedly. Dahlberg shares Whitman's incantory manner, his free verse, and his catalogue technique; but he qualifies Whitman's primitivism and is skeptical of his spontaneity and his commonality. His description of Whitman focuses on the sensual qualities of Whitman's work and on his essentially mystical demeanor:

There was a man named Walt Whitman,
Prophetic goat and Buddha of the states,
An evangelist of the rank gullet,
And the pagan works of Phallus.
An Old Testament Balaam was he,
And as lickerous as the Angels
Who parted the thighs of the daughters of men. (45)

What Dahlberg admires most about Whitman is not his poetic manner but his plea that men should not be separated from each other. Whitman's mass "I" means for Dahlberg the connection between men and man, the humanity we all share. He sees Whitman as the American Adam, the new man of the New World, singing a song of hope and optimism. However, since we have surely not taken Whitman's message to heart, the poem ends with the despairing line, "Whitman, our Adam, has died in our loins" (46).

The two parables which follow the Whitman poem are reminiscent of the parables which conclude *The Flea of Sodom.* Neither is successful as poetry, and the second is particularly puzzling. A "delicate man" is advised to "Sow anger and bitter leaves by quiet waters" (47). He is also admonished to "fear most the knowledge of the evening wolves," and is given additional equally enigmatic advice. He asks if the person proffering the advice is a seer, and the speaker replies "O my Bitterness, I am the SHAME Crying out of the Ground" (47). As Dahlberg himself remarks in the opening pages of *Can These Bones Live,* "Resolve these ambiguities, who can?"

A poem on the Mississippi entitled "Mechassipi," preserving a phonetic rendering of the Indian name for the river, is one of the more successful longer poems in the collection. The river, as is often the case in Dahlberg's work, is symbolic of many things—the origins of man, that knowledge which we seek, the continuity of human life. He makes this symbolic connection early in the poem:

Man cannot achieve knowledge
Except what water yields to mortal mind.
Truths are in the bitter marshes of the deceased.
The secret of the Kosmos is not in the earth.

Heed the inland water oracles
For ease and pleasant chance,

> But for the limitless journey to source
> Go to the saline depths. (48)

The poem relates the continuity of the river to the eternal suffering of man. Suffering, for Dahlberg, is a requisite of himan nature; and man's feeble attempts to relieve his burden are doomed to failure. Yet, paradoxically, as Dahlberg has stated again and again in *The Sorrows of Priapus* and *The Carnal Myth,* in these attempts man defines his humanity—that which elevates him from the animals. If we take away his inquisitive spirit, his thirsting after knowledge, man becomes one with the beasts. We must become aware of our limitations, but not necessarily submit to them. As Dahlberg concludes the poem,

> We are cartographers,
> Unheeding the singing maggots
> If bereft of the Angel.
> Study and be still in the month of rains. (51)

"Six Percent," a departure from most of the poems in this collection, is an attack on usury and human greed, which is certainly consistent with much of Dahlberg's writing, but in addition it is an attack on the religions of man which he depicts as materialistic and despotic. The priests of the world Dahlberg describes as "Midianite princes, / In black flowing clergyman trousers. / Concealing the belly and thighs of the beast . . ." (52). The poem is one of the most savagely satirical of those in the collection, and it is very different in tone, manner, and execution from anything else Dahlberg has written.

As I have already suggested, the fourteen short poems which conclude the volume are more personal in nature than the earlier poems; they are closer to the spirit of *Because I Was Flesh* than to that of *The Sorrows of Priapus.* The themes of human suffering, of man's apartness, of his inability to transcend his bestiality—all are still present—but, they are present in a more personal sense, they reveal themselves through Dahlberg's own experience. This personal quality gives the poems a greater concreteness and specificity than the earlier work, and for this reason they elicit a more intense emotional reaction from the reader.

Ten of these later poems are dedicated to William M. Ryan,

former Chairman of the English Department of the University of Missouri at Kansas City where Dahlberg taught in 1965 as a visiting professor; and there are four untitled poems which conclude the volume. The subjects of the Ryan poems are familiar. There is a complaint about the necessities of the flesh, and a poem on aging which begin the sequence. This second poem, like the final stanza of "Sing in the Beginning," is a deeply felt expression of a writer who feels his powers are waning but continues to write in search of a "literary" immortality. "I wither simply to hire fame and a decent headstone, / And may my grave not be vexed with the wretched gift I bring it" (54).

The third poem in this series attempts to express Dahlberg's concept of the relation of the individual to the cosmos, and it has an oddly metaphysical manner. The close relationship between love and death—the "metaphysical shudder" so often expressed by John Donne and George Herbert—is here concisely, if somewhat paradoxically, evoked: "When I am mewed up in a casket / My bones will be as lecherous as they are now" (55). This poem is followed by one on the passage of time and by another on the degree to which men have abandoned their cultural heritage. This poem signals a shift in the intention of the sequence, as it and the two poems which follow are divorced from personal concerns. The sixth verse is a catalogue of mythological names; the seventh is an attack on modern "trades," a poem which would be humorous if Dahlberg did not mean it so seriously: "Woe to the bookkeeper for he keeps an account of another man's avarice" (59). The eighth poem in the section is a specific attack on the trade which seems to horrify Dahlberg most—New York's garment industry.

Finally, in the last two poems of the sequence, Dahlberg returns to personal experience for subject matter. The first is a surprisingly tender poem about his father—particularly surprising when we recall the depiction of Saul, Dahlberg's father, in *Because I Was Flesh.* After condemning Saul in the autobiography, Dahlberg writes that "The sweat of my father is my wafer and wine. / I keep his ghost within my breast, / For when he lived I wounded him" (61). The last poem in the series, "February 18," is dedicated to Lizzie Dahlberg, and it seems to be an expression of Dahlberg's feelings upon learning of his mother's death.

The four poems which conclude the volume seem unrelated.

There is a poem on Dahlberg's restlessness; one which very accurately captures the fervor of Dahlberg's search for meaningful human relationships; another, a long one, on New York; and a final poem about the superiority of the primitive life to modern existence. The second poem in this series is worth quoting in its entirety because it perfectly pinpoints Dahlberg's continuing dilemma: his plea that man not live in isolation from other men, yet his inability to relate to other people and form lasting relationships:

I am galled and stung and wonder why.
I am genial by accident,
Gray and hulled as the sea at noon,
And by evening rueful as a ditch
With no twilight to salve my bruised gorge.
When I am in the sun
The arrows of the moon pierce my bosom.
I put on the colors of my nature
As the woman her powder and paint,
And would not know I was bad or choleric
Were there no people to affect my spleen.
Were there no persons in the earth
I would have no faults.
I could be content to embrace a rock, a precipice or a ravine,
Could I do without others.
Were I a sandy bank,
Or were there bedrock to bottom my identity,
I would not be my own enemy. (64)

## III The Leafless American

A word about this collection of "fourteen works of belles-lettres" completes our survey of the Dahlberg canon. Edited by Harold Billings, *The Leaflless American* brings together a number of previously uncollected Dahlberg pieces written mostly during the 1950's. An excellent introduction by Billings perfectly pinpoints the origins of the Dahlberg style: "Dahlberg's words are shaped in a matrix of winds from the four geographic corners of his sensibility: the Hellenic, the Hebraic, the American primitive-pastoral, and what he would perhaps term his own personal 'Pulse.'"[7] From the Hellenic aspects of Dahlberg's sensibility comes the concern for order, proportion, hierarchy, and his reverence for the Classics; from the Hebraic comes his intense moralism, his insistence on proper and decorous human conduct, and his awareness of human limitations. From the American primitive-pastoral, a tradition which surely includes Thoreau and Whitman, comes his faith in the natural and consequently his disdain for the artificial and his yearning for simplicity. And from his own personal "pulse" comes that which makes Dahlberg's writing more than simply the sum of all these traditions—a deep awareness of human suffering derived from the personal experience of his troublesome life.

The title poem, "The Leafless American," is basically a recasting of passages from *The Sorrows of Priapus* into verse paragraphs which may serve to emphasize, as Billings notes in the introduction, that Dahlberg's prose is often "only a jot away from poetry" (viii). Dahlberg has rearranged the sentences and has made some additions and deletions, but his message is the same as in the earlier book: man must rediscover his origins, his connection to the land, and abandon his cities if he is to flourish. In *The Sorrows,* he writes: "Whatever we do is vast, unconscious geography; we are huge giants of the mesa. The prairie is still an altar for the coyote and Ishmael" (63). In the poem he elaborates somewhat, but the thought is the same: "Whatever we do is vast, unconscious geography; we are huge space giants of the mesa, surd, mad rivers that rush along, and we do not care to be near each other; this is not ancient wickedness, but solitary prairie grazing" (2). Other passages are taken directly from *The Sorrows* without any alteration.

Billings regards the essay "A Decline of Souls" as one of the major essays of Dahlberg's career" (ix). In the sense that it serves as a synthesis of all of Dahlberg's major themes, Billings is certainly correct. The quotation from Amiel which precedes the essay captures its main points concisely: " '*The statistician will register a growing progress, and the moralist a gradual decline: on the one hand, a progress of things; on the other a decline of souls. The useful will take the place of the beautiful, industry of art, . . . and arithmetic of poetry. The spleen will become the malady of a levelling age*' " (6).

The idea that a progress of things often means a decline of souls is central to Dahlberg's thought, and the idea developed in this essay shows how this dialectic is particularly true of the "progress" of America. The modern American is the victim of the merchant and the state. Propagandized by both of these evils, he is "duped by the puritan gospel of work" (7) and becomes a "pragmatical slave of the immoral corporation" (8). Directed and victimized by these impersonal forces, the American has lost sight of what it means to be human: "Afraid of touching anybody lest he be infected by a germ, he is unable to catch the most important of all human diseases, affection" (9). Modern man's central concern is to accumulate things. Our abundance has made us insatiable and has complicated our lives immensely. Dahlberg cites an ancient Chinese proverb as the essence of his credo: "If you have two loaves of bread, sell one, and buy a lily" (12). Man must discover beauty and human affection if he is to survive. We Americans are a long way from doing so, and "our history is the tragedy of separation" (15). If the reader is looking for a summary of all of Dahlberg's most deeply held convictions, this essay is a major source.

The next two essays are about places particularly meaningful to Dahlberg's own experience—Kansas City and Spain, with particular reference to Mallorca. American writers, he comments in the first, are always nostalgic about the places of their past. His evocation of Kansas City attempts to avoid this stumbling block. Dahlberg admits he hates Kansas City, but it is so deeply imbedded in his experiences that he is continually drawn to it: "It is buried deep down in the loamy cairn of identity in which one can plant everything without going anywhere"(26). The essay on Mallorca, entitled "Tears of the Virgin," is more rambling and touches on many aspects of Spanish culture with emphasis on the enormous power of the church.

In "Rome and America," Dahlberg points out analogies between the decline of the Roman Empire and modern America. The main difference, as he sees it, is that America did not even develop a civilization before it began to decline: "America has produced no annalist to be placed alongside Livy, Suetonius, Gibbon or Jacob Burckhardt. What is conspicuous in Parkman, Prescott, and the Spanish discoverer chroniclers is not intellectual faculty, but energy" (40). But even our energy is being dissipated and wasted in our insane quest for material progress. Discussing the reign of Diocletian, Dahlberg remarks, "he had almost as morbid a passion for building as the chancellor of a U.S.A. university"(40).

"How do you Spell Fool?" is a bitter reply to Edouard Roditi's review of *The Flea of Sodom* which appeared in *Poetry* magazine. A classic example of Dahlberg's invective at its harshest, it is the kind of essay that will not win Dahlberg many readers, although he counters each of Roditi's objections with facility. "The Malice of Witlings" is an indictment of contemporary book reviewers in general and it is much more tempered and effective than the reply to Roditi. Again objecting to the cult of the original in modern letters, Dahlberg writes, "One celebrated noddy of our times exclaims, make it new, but I say, make it human"(51).

The essay on Stephen Crane presents a very complimentary view of Crane, although Dahlberg finds *The Red Badge of Courage* "too preachy." He admires "The Blue Hotel," "The Open Boat," "The Bride Comes to Yellow Sky," and "The Five White Mice." Dahlberg's fondness for Crane is based on what he feels is Crane's ability to recapture the American terrain—his closeness to the land. "Crane was our pioneer terrain; he was Colorado, New Mexico, the mesquite, the Sierra Madre"(59).

Sherwood Anderson is also treated affectionately in Dahlberg's essay on *Mid-American Chants,* which was written originally as a preface to a new edition of that work. Anderson, one of Dahlberg's mentors, is seen as "an unaffected, artless singer, a midwestern child of the muses"(64). Dahlberg feels that, like Crane, Anderson knew America well and had a consciousness of place which invigorates all his writing.

A review of Oscar Wilde's *De Profundis* which is critical of Wilde's hedonism and his "intellectual perversion" is followed by a revaluation of Nietzsche based on Dahlberg's reading of Walter Kaufmann's *Nietzsche*. Kaufmann's book, according to Dahlberg, rescues Nietzsche from years of misinterpretation. Nietzsche teaches us "to ascend the moral mountains"(74), and we must examine the totality of his achievement before we pass judgment.

"Methuselah's Funeral" is the most unusual work in the collection. A generic experiment, it is perhaps most accurately categorized as a fable. It seems closely related to a work Dahlberg has often spoken highly of: Christopher Smart's "Rejoice in the Lamb." Dahlberg constructs an elaborate scripture complete with genealogy, parable, prayer, and advice. The rub is that the scripture concerns cats rather than men. He begins: "This is the book of the Cat Sin which was written by the cat men and women of

New Topeth, an island village that lies in the sand dunes of Hinnom. These are Ham's descendants of whom it is told, idleness begat sloth, which produced malice that begat the Cat Sin. What issue has Cat Adam? Adam bare Seth who married his Angora sister, and they bare Maltese-Angora Enoch"(75). It is difficult to make anything of this fragment, which is clever enough, but which is also often opaque and undecipherable. Many biblical characters are described as one sort of cat or another, and there are certainly references to the state of modern man; but, beyond these obvious connections, "Methuselah's Funeral" remains cryptic.

A long poem entitled "The Garment of Ra" and an essay entitled "The Sandals of Judith" complete the collection. Thematically and stylistically, both are reminiscent of *The Sorrows of Priapus.* The poem restates Dahlberg's continuing search for man's origins; and the Cain-Abel myth is again central to Dahlberg's conception as it is in so many of the poems in *Cinpango's Hinder Door.* In stanza thirteen, there is a clear explication of Dahlberg's symbolic use of this myth; and it may shed some light on many of the poems in the earlier work:

> Man together is Abel, and apart he is Cain,
> For Abel is the kin of every broken hope,
> And the blood that flows in a single vein.
> The vows lie beneath the pecking rains,
> December is lament,
> Twigs and green are summer's ruse,
> The swallow and robin laugh,
> And Cain forgets Adam's bones.
> Guard the dead lest all be Cain. (95)

When we forget our common origins, we separate from one another and destroy one another. We must preserve the past, "guard the dead," or we will destroy the present, "lest all be Cain." In the essay, the theme from *The Sorrows* is man's bestiality and sensuality, a note struck in the very first sentence: "More towns and cities are destroyed by sexual disorders than by plagues, famine, and disease"(97). Like Holofernes, who "lost his life because the sandals that Judith was wearing deprived him of all his senses"(102), man's libido drives him constantly to irrationality—if not to the edge of insanity.

In all, *The Leafless American* is a valuable addition to Dahlberg's works; but it contributes little new direction to his over-all development. We have come across almost all of these ideas before in other works, but this collection corroborates the conception of Dahlberg as a generic innovator, and it presents us with a useful summary of his major themes and ideas. The essay "A Decline of Souls" particularly is an excellent summary of the Dahlberg "credo," and it may serve as a concise introduction to his work after 1940.

CHAPTER *10*

# The Achievement

I BEGAN this survey of Edward Dahlberg's writing with the suggestion that a critical work about a living author is a hazardous and uncertain undertaking. Certainly the most hazardous part of the venture is the attempt to summarize his contribution—to place his work within the confines of an ongoing literary tradition. A book about a writer is in a sense a testimony to his achievement, a monument to his works; but we must surely be wary of constructing that monument while the work is still in progress. As I write this essay, Dahlberg is at work on a collection of texts dealing with the discovery and exploration of the Americas, tentatively entitled *The Gold of Ophir.* In addition, he is contemplating a novella and a new book for Weybright and Talley entitled *The Colossal Dwarfs.* All of these works in progress hint at still more generic experimentation, and it is impossible to determine at this stage in his career whether or not his best work is yet before him. The recent appearance of *The Confessions of Edward Dahlberg* has clearly demonstrated that his creative powers remain forceful and that any attempt to construct an "overview" of the Dahlberg canon at this time would be an exercise in futility.

Yet the work we do have is already a formidable achievement, and it should have earned Dahlberg a more secure literary reputation than he currently enjoys. Despite the shortcomings we may find in individual works, few could dispute the fact that the totality of the work is an impressive body of literature and one which has greatly contributed to and enriched our literary tradition in the twentieth century. Dahlberg's work reveals to us a masterful prose stylist, a man who has devoted the major part of his life to the *art* of writing; and for this reason alone his work merits our careful attention.

In his introduction to *The Edward Dahlberg Reader,* Paul Carroll comments quite accurately about Dahlberg's style: "Certainly there is no prose like Dahlberg's prose in all of American literature. At its best the Dahlberg style is monumental and astonishing" (xiii). Even Dahlberg's detractors agree with Carroll's judgment, for Dahlberg's style *is* unique, monumental, and astonishing; but it is ironically these very characteristics which, it seems to me, have limited its appeal. They perhaps provide a clue to the reasons that Dahlberg's work has not yet reached a wide audience and that we still find his name on lists of "the most neglected contemporary writers." For Dahlberg's prose is "monumental and astonishing" because his lines are pulsing with resonances from the world's literature and myth. Few readers are able to bring to his work the enormous repository of referents he seems to demand, and almost everyone who writes about Dahlberg apologizes at some point or another (and let me do so here) for the limitations of background which place a full understanding and assimilation of Dahlberg's many esoteric allusions beyond his grasp. But the difficulty of the prose is hardly in and of itself sufficient reason for the relatively limited audience his work has reached. Certainly "difficult" and allusive writers are no rarity in the twentieth century; indeed, Joyce, Eliot, and Pound, the triumverate of twentieth-century literary sensibility, managed to turn difficulty into a literary virtue.

I think we must turn to the other characteristic implicit in Carroll's remarks for a more sufficient reason for Dahlberg's limited popularity, namely his "uniqueness." In a very real sense, he is a man out of his time, a voice speaking to us from another age; and it may be extremely difficult for some readers to make the necessary adjustments. For Dahlberg's models we must look to the Elizabethans, and even more to the geniuses of the baroque seventeenth-century prose style—Robert Burton, Sir Thomas Browne, John Donne—rather than to what we have come to accept as the models of "good writing" in our own century. The prose of Ernest Hemingway, for example, which is often cited as the epitome of clear, concise, effective prose style, is for Dahlberg the essence of bad writing, of vulgarity, and of the "decline" of language in our time. The books which lie behind his own work are Donne's *Devotions on Emergent Occasions,* Browne's *Urn-Burial* and *Religio Medici,* and, most of all, Burton's *Anatomy of Melancholy*—not *The Sun Also Rises, The Great Gatsby,* or *The Grapes of Wrath.* Thus Dahlberg asks from his readers a wholly different set of literary values than they often possess, and an appreciation of his prose takes a good deal of reconditioning.

I have been aiming my remarks here primarily at Dahlberg's work since 1940, but it seems to me there is a good deal of literary value, if not stylistic value, in the early novels as well. *Bottom Dogs* is an exemplary "novel of the streets," and it had a major impact on a particular kind of American fiction for the next two decades. *From Flushing to Calvary,* though less widely known, seems to me an important work because it brings together two major literary currents of the 1930's—the proletarian and the psychological. A novel of the streets, as is *Bottom Dogs,* it is more experimental, less conventional, and, in my judgment, more effective. Even *Those Who Perish,* which is in many ways Dahlberg's least successful book, is a superlative example of the novel as social criticism, and it illustrates the intense social conscience which Dahlberg and other writers of the period brought to the fiction of the 1930's. If Dahlberg had stopped writing at the end of the "depression decade," his work would still deserve a place, if minor, in the literary history of our time.

Of course, the fact that he did not stop writing makes that place a good deal more significant because Dahlberg's major achievement begins with the conclusion of his "proletarian" period. But the books after *Those Who Perish* are much more complex than the earlier work, and they present problems of a very different kind for the literary historian or critic. These problems, it seems to me, are basically of two kinds: those related to Dahlberg's work and those which primarily concern his life. We can fairly argue (and indeed most twentieth-century "analytic" critics have) that a man's life be kept apart from his work and that we should look only at the esthetic value of the work in reaching our judgments. But this critical pose is one that Dahlberg has attacked severely in almost all of his critical writing; and, if we are to evaluate his work as he would evaluate others, a consideration of biographical details is imperative. The man and the work are one, he has so often argued; and it is folly to try to separate the two.

The problems which grow out of Dahlberg's work are primarily those of inconsistency and intolerance. His literary criticism particularly is difficult to accept without reservations because he disparages most contemporary writers with an invective that often shocks or amuses more than it convinces. Running through much of his criticism are attacks on writers to whom he apparently owes a debt, and for failings his work has in common with theirs. He attacks Joyce and Eliot for the extensive allusions in their work, yet few writers cite other authors more extensively than Dahlberg himself. He is always impatient with writers or critics overly concerned with "art" or "esthetics," but is himself an extremely conscious and conscientious craftsman who works and reworks his material for esthetic effect. He emphasizes the need for American writers to know the land, yet he has spent a good deal of his life abroad and is among the most peripatetic of contemporary authors. He disparages the "cult of originality" in American letters, while he is an extremely original writer, despite his emphasis on the literature of the past.

The list could be continued, but these paradoxes should serve to corroborate the impression that Dahlberg's criticism is enigmatic and that his literary practice is often at odds with his critical theory. This inconsistency is reflective of the enigma of Dahlberg the man as well as Dahlberg the critic, and it is perhaps a measure of his total character that his inconsistencies are quite consistent. In part, these paradoxes may be accepted and understood as a result of his self-imposed isolation from other writers. For, while he seems to believe that American literature has suffered greatly because our writers have worked apart from one another with little sense of community or comradeship, there are few modern writers who have been so unable to sustain any lasting personal relationships. With very few exceptions, almost all of Dahlberg's friendships have ended in bitter disputes.

Yet, despite all of these disparities, Dahlberg's critical work is well worth pondering because it can enable us to view a great many writers in a new light, apart from the stereotyped dictates of conventional criticism. His moralistic critical stance is a startling contrast to the analytically oriented criticism of our time; but, as such, it may shake us loose from our preconceptions and broaden our critical perspective. Like his prose style, his critical point of view is reflective of a past age, rather than of our own, but if Dahlberg's work has any single point it is that the past is almost always worth listening to.

This orientation toward the past is the basis of another of Dahlberg's contributions—his recovery of our native mythological heritage. We have become so accustomed to think of myths as the exclusive property of the Classical period that those which are native to the American land and experience remain largely unknown to us. *The Sorrows of Priapus* and *The Carnal Myth,* whatever shortcomings the reader may find in them, are books which go a long way toward correcting this condition. They are rich repositories of native lore and are revelations of a cultural tradition which we certainly need to know more about.

In the final analysis, however, it is difficult to quarrel with the contention that Dahlberg's literary reputation to the present must rest primarily upon the accomplishment of his two major works, *Can These Bones Live* and *Because I Was Flesh.* The former teaches us that the writing of literary criticism at its very best is as creative an act as the writing of fiction, poetry, or drama. Literature is the starting point of *Can These Bones Live*; but the book is ultimately more than the sum of its parts and one which, as Dahlberg would put it, can help reveal ourselves to us. Its startling insights into the major works of our literary tradition enable us to perceive important connections between diverse literary works and return to us a tradition much enriched and made more meaningful. *Because I Was Flesh* is the summit of Dahlberg's achievement because it fuses the poles of his sensibility—the mythological and the personal—into a work of self-revelation that expresses what it means to be *human* as well as what it means to be Edward Dahlberg.

This fusion of the universal and the particular lies at the very core of Dahlberg's best writing, and it relates him directly to the mainstream of the American tradition. We can think of William Faulkner, who creates a world of universal dimensions but, at the same time, gives us a carefully detailed "realistic" portrayal of a Mississippi county; or of Theodore Dreiser, who painstakingly chronicles the life of Clyde Griffiths but ultimately creates a story that is concerned with forces that Dreiser saw as fundamental to human life—man's impotency in shaping his own destiny; or even of Nathaniel Hawthorne, who can tell us a good deal about the manners and customs of a Colonial New England town while he is, at the same time, intensely interested in illustrating the perennial themes of man's existence—evil, sin, death, love.

But, if there is any American writer Dahlberg most resembles, it is Herman Melville, who, like Dahlberg, was an extremely individualistic man, an iconoclast, a nay-sayer, and a rebel against the accepted values of his age. Dahlberg shares Melville's lack of familial security (*vide Pierre*), his "baroque" prose style, his concern for primitive myth and ritual (*Omoo, Typee,* and *Mardi*), his isolation as a writer ("Bartleby the Scrivener"), his criticism of the age in which he was born (*The Confidence Man*), and his extensive world travels. Like Dahlberg, Melville had an extremely limited readership during his lifetime. After two commercially successful books, he sank into obscurity, and his major achievements—*Moby Dick, Pierre, The Confidence Man*—were comparatively unnoticed.

It is, of course, too early to know whether Dahlberg will continue to follow the Melvillian pattern. In any case, such comparisons are only suggestive and are not intended to "define" a literary career. Already Dahlberg has received the recognition that Melville never had during his lifetime. Most of Dahlberg's works since 1941 are still in print; and *Can These Bones Live, Alms for Oblivion, Because I Was Flesh,* and *The Edward Dahlberg Reader* have all been reissued in paperback editions which are beginning to reach a wider audience. As more readers become familiar with the almost unprecedented scope of Dahlberg's accomplishment, I have little doubt that his literary reputation will continue to grow. When we consider the great diversity of Dahlberg's writing, his generic innovation and invention, his strengths as a novelist, a mythographer, a literary critic, an autobiographer, an aphorist and poet, we may begin to bestow the respect and acclaim that this unique American writer so clearly has earned.

# Notes and References

## *Chapter One*

1. T. S. Eliot, *Selected Essays* (New York, 1950), p. 4.
2. Ihab Hassan, "The Sorrows of Edward Dahlberg," *The Massachusetts Review,* V (Spring, 1964), 459.
3. *Epitaphs of our Times* (New York, 1967), p. 86.
4. *Because I Was Flesh* (New York, 1964), p. 1.
5. *Ibid.,* p. 8.
6. *Epitaphs of our Times,* p. 21.
7. *Ibid.,* p. 22.
8. Harold Billings, ed., *Edward Dahlberg: American Ishmael of Letters* (Austin, Texas, 1968), p. 15.
9. Quoted in *The Nation,* CXCVIII (March 30, 1964), 331.
10. *Epitaphs of our Times,* p. 22.
11. The details of Dahlberg's various marriages are obscure. He mentions a previous marriage (or marriages) in *Because I Was Flesh* and in *The Confessions of Edward Dahlberg.* In neither case does he name the woman. There are at least two subsequent marriages on record: to R'lene Howell in 1950 and to Julia Lawlor in 1967.
12. Edouard Roditi, "Prophet or Pedant," *Poetry,* LXXVII (Jan., 1951), 236–38.
13. *Epitaphs of our Times,* p. 104.
14. Hassan, p. 457.
15. Letter dated Jan. 23, 1956. I am grateful to Edwin Seaver of George Braziller & Co. for permitting me access to the file of Dahlberg's letters.
16. Letter dated April 11, 1958.
17. Fred Moramarco, "An Interview with Edward Dahlberg," *Western Humanities Review,* XX (Summer, 1966), 252–53.
18. *Epitaphs of our Times,* p. 144.
19. Alfred Kazin, *On Native Grounds* (New York, 1942), p. 382.
20. Alfred Kazin, "The Eloquence of Failure," *The Reporter,* XXXI (August 13, 1964), 62.

*Chapter Two*

1. Walter Rideout, *The Radical Novel in the United States* (Cambridge, Mass., 1956), p. 166.
2. Quoted in Jonathan Williams, "Edward Dahlberg's Book of Lazarus," *Texas Quarterly*, VI (Summer, 1963), 38.
3. *Bottom Dogs* (San Francisco, 1961), p. 207. All subsequent quotations from *Bottom Dogs* are from this edition.
4. D. H. Lawrence, *Sons and Lovers* (London, 1913), p. 259.
5. *From Flushing to Calvary* (New York, 1932), p. 21. All subsequent quotations from *From Flushing to Calvary* refer to this edition.
6. Moramarco, p. 249.
7. In Braziller collection of letters.

*Chapter Three*

1. "Hitler's Power over Germany: The Nazi Strength Analyzed," New York *Times*, April 9, 1933, p. 2.
2. Moramarco, p. 253.
3. Kenneth Fearing, *Poems* (New York, 1936), p. 14.
4. See Williams, p. 40.
5. *Those Who Perish* (New York, 1934), p. 46. Subsequent quotations from *Those Who Perish* are from this edition.
6. Moramarco, p. 253.
7. Kazin, "Eloquence of Failure," p. 52.
8. This sense of frustration and moral outrage is a major note in the literature of social protest. The resemblance between this quotation and the following passage from William Dean Howells' *A Hazard of New Fortunes* may further illustrate Dahlberg's relation to this tradition. Howells writes: "and so we go on, pushing and pulling, climbing and crawling, thrusting aside and trampling underfoot; lying, cheating, stealing; and when we get to the end, covered with blood and dirt and sin and shame, and look back over the way we've come to a palace of our own, or the poor house . . . I don't think the retrospect can be pleasing." (New York, 1960), p. 378.
9. Henry Hart, ed., *American Writers' Congress* (New York, 1935), pp. 10–11.
10. *Ibid.*, p. 26.
11. *Ibid.*, p. 28.
12. *Ibid.*, p. 32.
13. *Ibid.*
14. *Ibid.*, p. 180.
15. *Ibid.*, pp. 108–9.
16. *Signature* (Spring, 1936), unpaged.

17. *Ibid.*
18. *Ibid.*

## Chapter Four

1. Allen Tate, "A Great Stylist: The Prophet as Critic," *Sewanee Review,* LXVIX (Spring, 1961), 314.
2. Billings, p. 18.
3. *Can These Bones Live* (Ann Arbor, 1967), p. 3. All future quotations from this work are from this edition. Perhaps it is worth noting here the same passage from the first edition of *Do These Bones Live* to suggest the kind of stylistic changes Dahlberg made for the later edition. There are three changes, all in the direction of conciseness and accuracy. After the word "bound" in the opening sentence, the first edition has a semi-colon and continues, "the closer we look the more difficult it is to distinguish one from the other." In the later edition, Dahlberg wisely decided to let the image speak for itself. In place of the phrase "embitters the earth," the first edition has "galls bitterness," which is surely less precise. And the final allusion ("let me look into," etc.) is attributed to Kropotkin in *Do These Bones Live,* while there is no source given in the later edition. See *Do These Bones Live* (New York, 1941), p. 3.
4. Tate, p. 317.
5. Williams, p. 45.
6. (New York, 1960). Fiedler nowhere cites Dahlberg in his work, but their remarks on women in our literature are quite similar.
7. Billings, p. 18.
8. Williams, p. 35.
9. *Ibid.*, p. 46.
10. William Carlos Williams, "The Flea of Sodom," in Billings, p. 56.
11. *Ibid.*, p. 61.
12. *Ibid.*, p. 62.
13. *Ibid.*
14. Moramarco, p. 249.

## Chapter Five

1. *The Carnal Myth* (New York, 1968), p. 11. Subsequent quotations, later in this chapter from *The Carnal Myth* are from this edition.
2. *The Sorrows of Priapus* (Norfolk, Conn., 1957), viii. All quotations from *The Sorrows* are from this edition.
3. *Reasons of the Heart* (New York, 1965), p. 23.
4. See Chapter 4, note 14.
5. In Billings, pp. 67–82.

6. Edmund White, "The Dahlberg Dilemma," *The New Republic,* LCIX (August 3, 1968), 20.

7. Josephine Herbst, "Edward Dahlberg's *Because I Was Flesh,*" *Southern Review,* I, New Series (April, 1965), 340.

8. *Book World* (June 2, 1968), p. 6.

9. Edmund White, *op. cit.,* p. 19, comments on this "irritating" aspect of Dahlberg's style. White cites the following passage: "Epical companionship is the hymn of Ares; it is battle and strife; one must be as prepared for truth, love, or a friend, as Diomedes was ready at all times for rapine, sleeping on a hard bed with upright spears planted near enough to grasp them. Chrysostom said that the Thebans bore the marks of spears on their bodies, which had been left by the dragon's teeth Cadmus had sown." White remarks, "In this passage, Chrysostom's remark is obviously hitching a free ride, but the addition garbles the entire point Dahlberg was making. Similarly, he tells us, 'The Scythians carried all their laws in their heads, having no need of books,' and then throws in for good measure, 'The plays of Terence are about gluttons and parasites, but the Scythians, being too poor to have either, did not require Roman comedies,' Full stop. New paragraph. Terence, like a movie star in a gossip column, has had his 'mention' and will not appear again in the book."

10. Paul Carroll, ed., *The Edward Dahlberg Reader* (New York, 1967), p. 307.

*Chapter Six*

1. David Daiches, *Critical Approaches to Literature* (Englewood Cliffs, New Jersey, 1956), p. 39.

2. *Truth Is More Sacred* (New York, 1961), p. 169. All future quotations from this work are from this edition.

3. In a letter to Stanley Burnshaw, Dahlberg writes, "I don't like Robert Graves, and refused to shake hands with him when I was in Mallorca some time in 1954 because I thought he was an ambitious charlatan. Read had expressed great reluctance even to write about him. Graves had attacked Read, and the latter said that he did not consider Graves worthy of being included in our book. I replied that I didn't think Pound and Eliot were either, but that we had certain didactic tasks to perform, and that we had to be of use to students and to apprentices in literature." *Epitaphs of our Times,* p. 276.

4. Herbst, p. 348.

5. *Alms for Oblivion* (Minneapolis, 1964), p. viii. All subsequent quotations from *Alms for Oblivion* are from this edition.

6. *Bottom Dogs,* p. iii.

7. For a more extended account of Dahlberg's friendship with

Crane, see his memoir, "Hart Crane," *New York Review of Books* (Jan. 20, 1966), pp. 19–22.

8. Frank MacShane, "Two Reviews," in Billings, p. 122.

### *Chapter Seven*

1. Herbst, pp. 342–43.
2. Kazin, "Eloquence of Failure," p. 62.
3. Carroll, p. xiv.
4. *Because I Was Flesh* (New York, 1964), p. 4. Subsequent quotations are from this edition.
5. Braziller collection, Jan. 23, 1956.
6. *Ibid.*, Nov., 1959.
7. *Cinpango's Hinder Door* (Austin, Texas, 1965), p. 7.
8. Kazin, *loc. cit.*

### *Chapter Eight*

1. *The Confessions of Edward Dahlberg* (New York, 1971), p. vii. Subsequent quotations are from this edition.
2. Calvin Bedient, "Anyone's Miserable Chagrin," *New Republic* (February 6, 1971).
3. *Ibid.*, p. 32.

### *Chapter Nine*

1. MacShane in Billings, p. 124.
2. *Cinpango's Hinder Door* (Austin, Texas, 1965), p. 58. Subsequent quotations are from this edition.
3. *Reasons of the Heart* (New York, 1965), p. 9. Subsequent quotations are from this edition.
4. Herbst, p. 348.
5. MacShane in Billings, p. 127.
6. White, p. 19.
7. *The Leafless American* (Austin, Texas, 1967), p. vii. Subsequent quotations are from this edition.

# Selected Bibliography


PRIMARY SOURCES

1. *Books*

*Bottom Dogs.* London: G. P. Putnam's Sons, 1929. American edition: New York, Simon and Schuster, 1930. Paperback: San Francisco, City Lights, 1961.

*From Flushing to Calvary.* New York: Harcourt, Brace and Company, 1932.

*Kentucky Blue Grass Henry Smith.* Cleveland: White Horse Press, 1932. (Part Six of *From Flushing to Calvary* issued separately.)

*Those Who Perish.* New York: John Day Company, 1934.

*Do These Bones Live.* New York: Harcourt, Brace and Company, 1941.

*Sing O Barren.* London: George Routledge & Sons, 1947. (English edition of *Do These Bones Live,* revised.)

*The Flea of Sodom.* London: Peter Nevill Ltd., 1950. American edition: New York, New Directions, 1950.

*The Sorrows of Priapus.* Norfolk, Conn.: New Directions, 1957.

*Can These Bones Live.* New York: New Directions, 1960. (A completely revised edition of *Do These Bones Live* with drawings by James Kearns.) Paperback: Ann Arbor, University of Michigan Press, 1967.

*Truth Is More Sacred.* New York: Horizon Press, 1961. English edition: London, Routledge & Kegan Paul, 1961.

*Because I Was Flesh.* Norfolk, Conn.: New Directions, 1964. Paperback: New York, New Directions, 1967.

*Alms for Oblivion.* Minneapolis: University of Minnesota Press, 1964. Paperback: Minneapolis, University of Minnesota Press, 1967.

*Reasons of the Heart.* New York: Horizon Press, 1965.

*Cinpango's Hinder Door.* Austin: University of Texas Press, 1966.

*Epitaphs of Our Times. The Letters of Edward Dahlberg.* New York: George Braziller, 1967.

*The Edward Dahlberg Reader.* New York: New Directions, 1967. Paperback: New York, New Directions, 1967.

*The Leafless American.* Austin, Texas: Roger Beacham, 1967.

*The Carnal Myth.* New York: Weybright and Talley, 1968.

*The Confessions of Edward Dahlberg.* New York: George Braziller, 1971.

2. *Miscellaneous Writings*

"The Sick, the Pessimist, and the Philosopher," *The Occident,* LXXX (November, 1922), 141–44. Dahlberg's first published writing.

"Hitler's Power Over Germany: The Nazi Strength Analysed," New York *Times,* April 9, 1933, p. 3.

"Fascism & Writers." *American Writers' Congress.* Henry Hart (ed.). New York: International Publishers, 1935, pp. 26–32.

"Introduction." Kenneth Fearing. *Poems.* New York: Dynamo, 1936, pp. 11–14.

"Bitch Goddess: Notes on a Novel," *Signature* (Spring, 1936), unpaged.

"A Literary Correspondence," *Sewanee Review,* V (Spring–Summer, 1959), 177–82, 187–90, 198–203, 427–33, 439–41.

"Robert Graves and T. S. Eliot," *Twentieth Century,* CLXVI (August, 1959), 54–58.

"Because I Was Flesh, An Autobiography," *Sewanee Review,* LXVII (Fall, 1960), 548–64.

". . . and so my mother," *The Massachusetts Review,* III (Winter, 1962), 221–31.

"Essays & Poems: A Miscellany," *The Massachusetts Review,* V (Spring, 1964), 462–75.

"On Passions and Asceticism," *Sewanee Review,* LXXIII (Spring, 1965), 191–95.

"Adages," *Kenyon Review,* XXVII (Winter, 1965), 166.

"Hart Crane," *New York Review of Books,* V (January 20, 1966), 19–22.

"A Coruscation of Aphorisms," *Book World,* III (February 16, 1969), 6.

"Dahlberg on Dreiser, Anderson and Dahlberg," *New York Times Book Review* (January 31, 1971), pp. 2, 30–31.

Excerpts from Dahlberg's published works have also appeared in *New Directions in Prose and Poetry,* New York: New Directions, Numbers 12, 14, 15, 16, 17, and 19.

### SECONDARY SOURCES

This selected list of Dahlberg criticism does not include all the book reviews devoted to Dahlberg's work, but does list those that are most significant. For a more complete list of reviews of Dahlberg's books through *The Leafless American,* see under Billings listed below.

AARON, DANIEL. *Writers on the Left. Episodes in American Literary Communism.* New York: Harcourt, Brace and Company, 1961. Critical discussion of the writers of the 1930's. Dahlberg only briefly mentioned.

BEDIENT, CALVIN. "Anyone's Miserable Chagrin," *The New Republic,* CLXIV (February 6, 1971), 27–32. Negative review of *The Confessions.*

BILLINGS, HAROLD, ed. *Edward Dahlberg: American Ishmael of Letters.* Austin, Texas: Roger Beacham, 1968. Collection of the best essays devoted to Dahlberg's work to 1967. Several previously unpublished essays appear here, notably William Carlos Williams on *The Flea of Sodom,* Joseph Evans Slate on *The Sorrows of Priapus,* and Robert Kindrick on "Edward Dahlberg and Modern American Letters." Billings includes an extremely useful bibliography of reviews of Dahlberg's books on pages 164–67, as well as a lucid and concise Introduction to the Dahlberg canon.

———. *A Bibliography of Edward Dahlberg.* Austin, Texas: University of Texas Press, 1971. Comprehensive bibliography of all Dahlberg's published work. Includes a section on works about Dahlberg and updates the bibliography of reviews listed in the previous entry. Indispensable for any student of Dahlberg's work.

BOYLE, KAY. "A Man in the Wilderness," *The Nation,* CCIV (May 29, 1967), 693–94. Review of *Epitaphs of Our Times* and *The Edward Dahlberg Reader.*

CHAMETSKY, JULES. "Edward Dahlberg: Early and Late." Donald Madden (ed.). *Proletarian Writers of the Thirties.* Carbondale, Illinois: Southern Illinois University Press, 1968. Interesting comparison of the treatment of Dahlberg's subject matter in the early novels and in *Because I Was Flesh.*

DUNCAN, ROBERT. "Against Nature," *Poetry,* XCIV (April, 1959), 54–59. Negative but provocative review of *The Sorrows of Priapus.*

FARRELL, JAMES T. "In Search of the Image," *New Masses,* XIII (December 4, 1934), 21–22. Discussion of Dahlberg's "urban imagery" in the early novels.

FORD, FORD MADOX. "The Fate of the Semiclassic," *Forum,* XCVII (September, 1937), 126–28. Brief appreciation of Dahlberg's early work.

HASSAN, IHAB. "The Sorrows of Edward Dahlberg," *The Massachusetts Review,* V (Spring, 1964), 457–61. Sensitive reading of *Because I Was Flesh;* relates it to Dahlberg's earlier work.

HERBST, JOSEPHINE. "Edward Dahlberg's *Because I Was Flesh,*" *Southern Review,* I New Series (Spring, 1965), 337–51. Extended review of *Because I Was Flesh;* traces the development of Dahlberg's style.

HICKS, GRANVILLE *et al.* (eds.). *Proletarian Literature in the United States.* New York: International Publishers, 1935. Standard collection of the major proletarian writers of the 1930's.

KARLEN, ARNO. "The Wages of Risk," *The Nation,* CXCVIII (March 30, 1964), 331–34. Review of the reissue of *Bottom Dogs* and *Because I Was Flesh.*

KAZIN, ALFRED. "The Eloquence of Failure," *The Reporter,* XXXI (August 13, 1964), 59–62. Review of *Because I Was Flesh.*

———. *On Native Grounds. An Interpretation of Modern American Prose Literature.* New York: Reynal and Hitchcock, 1942. Standard survey of modern American prose; Dahlberg briefly mentioned.

KRAMER, HILTON. "The Confessions of Edward Dahlberg," *The New York Times Book Review* (January 31, 1971), pp. 1, 30–31. Review of *The Confessions.*

LIPTON, VICTOR. "Cudgels and Distaffs, for the Rebirth," *Prairie Schooner* (Winter, 1961), 286–88, 354–56. Review of the revised edition of *Can These Bones Live.*

MORAMARCO, FRED. "An Interview with Edward Dahlberg," *Western Humanities Review,* XX (Summer, 1966), 249–53. Conversation about Dahlberg's literary development.

RIDEOUT, WALTER. *The Radical Novel in the United States 1900–1954.* Cambridge, Masss.: Harvard University, 1956. Identifies Dahlberg as one of the originators of the "bottom dog" fiction of the 1930's.

RODITI, EDOUARD. "Prophet or Pedant," *Poetry,* LXXVII (January, 1951), 236–38. Caustic review of *The Flea of Sodom;* accuses Dahlberg of Fascist tendencies.

SHAPIRO, KARL. *To Abolish Children and Other Essays.* Chicago: Quadrangle Books, 1968. Casual discussion of Dahlberg's achievement.

SWADOS, HARVEY, ed. *The American Writer and the Great Depression.* New York: Bobbs-Merrill, 1966. Excellent selection of the literature of the 1930's; includes a section of *From Flushing to Calvary.*

TATE, ALLEN. "A Great Stylist: The Prophet as Critic," *Sewanee Review,* LXVIX (Spring, 1961), 314–17. Review of *Can These Bones Live.*

UNALI, LINA GAREGNANI. "Introduzione a Edward Dahlberg," *Studi Americani,* XI (1965), 271–308. Survey of Dahlberg's work by an Italian scholar.

WAIN, JOHN. "Eating Fables," *The New York Review of Books,* XI (January 2, 1969), 13–14. Review of *The Carnal Myth, The*

*Leafless American* and *Edward Dahlberg: American Ishmael of Letters.*

WHITE, EDMUND. "The Dahlberg Dilemma," *The New Republic,* LCIX (August 3, 1968), 19–21. Review of *The Carnal Myth* and *American Ishmael;* attempts to answer the question of "how Dahlberg got to be this way."

WHITTAKER, EDWARD KEITH. "Touching Pitch: A Reader's Garland for Edward Dahlberg." Unpublished master's thesis, Department of English, University of British Columbia, 1968. Lively survey of the Dahlberg canon; treats "all of Edward Dahlberg's work as one great book."

WILLIAMS, JONATHAN, ed. "A *Festschrift* for Edward Dahlberg," *TriQuarterly,* No. 19 (Fall, 1970). Entire issue devoted to an appreciation of Dahlberg's works by over sixty contemporary scholars, artists, and critics.

———. ed. *Edward Dahlberg: A Tribute.* New York: David Lewis, 1971. Reprint, in book form, of the *TriQuarterly Festschrift.*

———. "Edward Dahlberg's Book of Lazarus," *The Texas Quarterly,* VI (Summer, 1963), 35–49. Excellent introduction to Dahlberg's work up to *Because I Was Flesh.*

WILSON, EDMUND. *The Shores of Light.* New York: Farrar, Straus & Young, 1952. Wilson takes issue with Lawrence's Introduction to *Bottom Dogs.* He does not find the book repulsive, but, on the contrary, "gentle and unassertive."

# Index